NOT VERY QUIET

the anthology

I AM VERY QUIET

NOT VERY QUIET

the anthology

edited by
Moya Pacey and Sandra Renew

RECENT
WORK
PRESS

Not Very Quiet: the anthology
Recent Work Press
Canberra, Australia

Copyright © the authors, 2021

ISBN: 9780645180800 (paperback)

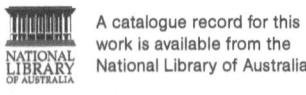
A catalogue record for this work is available from the National Library of Australia

All rights reserved. This book is copyright. Except for private study, research, criticism or reviews as permitted under the Copyright Act, no part of this book may be reproduced, stored in a retrieval system, or transmitted in any form by any means without prior written permission. Enquiries should be addressed to the publisher.

Cover image: from the New York City book campaign, 1919
Cover design: Recent Work Press
Set by Recent Work Press

recentworkpress.com

CONTENTS

Foreword *Sandra Renew, Moya Pacey* ix

Exposure *Cassandra Atherton* 1
this autistic guise *Oakley Ayden* 2
Rhythmic Oscillations *Magdalena Ball* 3
The camel and the straw *J V Birch* 5
Millennium *Wendy BooydeGraaff* 6
Out west *Emily Bourke* 7
Out in the open *Devika Brendon* 9
The art of costume *Michelle Brock* 11
Waiting on Imran Khan *Lisa Brockwell* 12
The Feminist *Denise Burton* 14
Malthus *Monica Carroll* 15
In one hundred days *Anne Casey* 16
I will fall sick if you photograph me *Jhilam Chattaraj* 17
Cheongsam *Eileen Chong* 19
Most Deadly *Emilie Collyer* 20
Tricks of the Trade *Jennifer Compton* 21
The dusky grasswren *PS Cottier* 23
Getting in the Way and Science *MTC Cronin* 24
Interior with wardrobe mirror *Jan Dean* 25
Scar massage *Tricia Dearborn* 26
On Joy Hester's late portraits of girls *Sally Denshire* 28
Black Dream Bird *Moyra Donaldson* 29
Our daily tread *Jane Downing* 30
A feast of a wardrobe *Natasha Dust* 31
The Strongest Girl in the World *Eugenie Edquist* 33

Spring Purples with Coast Tea Tree and Golden Wattle *Anne Elvey*	35
In half light *Diane Fahey*	36
At least I still remember *Amelia Fielden*	38
masque *Ellie Fisher*	39
Self-portrait in the Bathtub *Anna Forsyth*	40
Pointillism workshop at Gootchie, 1976 *Jane Frank*	41
Woman Quits Femininity *Irina Frolova*	43
All the willing hours *Kathryn Fry*	44
Christmas in November 2019 *Sophie Furlong Tighe*	45
Pandora's Kitchen *Allison Goldstein*	46
Noh *Hazel Hall*	47
Eating the Reef *Kristin Hannaford*	48
Wanted—Princess *Michelle Hartman*	50
Letter to a bride to be *Dominique Hecq*	51
The Sea Calls My Name *Gail Hennessy*	52
Where We Go *Jill Jones*	54
Hongoeka love poems *Michaela Keeble*	55
Oh! So Deliciously *Kathy Kituai*	57
Flora Cloth *Kimberly Lambright*	58
X300 *Robyn Lance*	59
Communion *Penelope Layland*	60
from the garlic wife *Nellie Le Beau*	61
A girl dies each night on TV *Wes Lee*	62
Playing dead *Rosanna E. Licari*	63
Just Before Covid-19 Hits I Sell My Gold *Miriam Wei Wei Lo*	64
A Secret Midtown Garden *LindaAnn LoSchiavo*	65
The crystal masks of Lynette and Donald *Kate Lumley*	66
Winged and killing after Catullus *Julie Maclean*	67

Disarming *Jacqui Malins*	68
Taking a picture *Sameeya Maqbool*	69
Abrasion *Jennifer Kemarre Martiniello*	70
Bodhi of a poem *Victoria McGrath*	71
In the Dutch tradition *Kate Miller*	72
Bartending *Rosalind Moran*	73
Diapause *Lizz Murphy*	74
Regent Theatres, Empire Halls *K A Nelson*	75
Camille Claudel *Gemma Nethercote Way*	76
August in Lahore *Nadia Niaz*	77
orderly queue *jenni nixon*	78
Watt and the onion *Jilly O'Brien*	79
A look that won't catch on *Denise O'Hagan*	80
I Do Remember the Wall *Rosa O'Kane*	81
The girl who said NO *Moya Pacey*	82
Nights with Arthur *Christine Paice*	83
There were coconuts *Anita Patel*	84
the space within a touch *Yvonne G Patterson*	85
To Ferry Landing *Sue Peachey*	86
Patterns Not Yet Possible *Meredith Pitt*	87
Ashridge Forest *Vanessa Proctor*	88
Trump and the Billionaires Play Dirty Pool in the Oval Office *Donna Pucciani*	89
Pocket Rocks *KA Rees*	90
Recovered *Sandra Renew*	92
Fallacy of the predicate *Sarah Rice*	93
Noli me tangere *Marka Rifat*	95
Eve Kosofsky Sedgwick Lunching Alone, 1987 *Danielle Rose*	96

20/20 *Michele Seminara*	97
woman in the lines *Ellen Shelley*	98
Folly *Melinda Smith*	99
In the Future, they Ate from Plates of Finest Porcelain *Abeir Soukieh*	100
The Wedding Suit *Gerry Stewart*	101
Waiting *Sarah St Vincent Welch*	102
The walk to school *Carmel Summers*	103
My father's mask *Robyn Sykes*	104
The Silk Roads *Lesley Synge*	105
Brisbane Water Estuary *Gillian Telford*	106
Reading the signs in FNQ *Helen Thurloe*	107
Species, Manifold *Catherine Trundle*	108
An olive rolls under the fridge *Anna Veprinska*	109
Cognates for a Floodplain *Maggie Wang*	110
Plastique in Brazil *Susan Wardell*	111
Alice *Jen Webb*	112
Hey Mister, you have devoured nearly all of it—this cake *Irene Wilkie*	113
Huhu *Sophia Wilson*	114
Straphanging *Jena Woodhouse*	115
Notes	116
Acknowledgements	118
Contributors	120

FOREWORD

When Moya Pacey, Tikka Wilson and I agreed to establish *Not Very Quiet* as a journal for women's poetry, we believed that despite many advancements for women there is still a gender bias operating in the poetry publishing world. I thought then, and still think now, that poetry, in all its traditional and new, evolving forms, is a critical production by women to help heal the ills and assaults of a world order that is not friendly or even benign to women. Over the eight published issues of NVQ we have seen women set out with something to say, crystallising the dissonance in the dominant discourses in a way that speaks to our readers, or indeed to anyone who is driven by revolution. In selecting the poems for each issue, we have found poetry which explores the complexities and possibilities of the human condition, the social constructions of gender in all its forms. We found poems that give expression to the social conscience of the community, including constructions of lesbian and queer, and the challenge this poses to the binaries (that is, the way we are used to thinking about gender only as either masculine or feminine) in the discourse and to issues of conflict and borders and boundaries. Our *Not Very Quiet* anthology includes many of these poems. Although we could not include all the great poems from the online issues, we hope you find the ones we have selected to be an inspirational and thought-provoking collection. —*Sandra Renew*

No-one could have foreseen what has happened in the world since we launched our very first issue of *Not Very Quiet* international women's poetry journal in September 2017. That issue coincided with the election of Donald Trump as President of the United States, and our initial provocation was to respond to Gloria Steinem's words from the Women's March on Washington after Trump's inauguration in January 2017. Since then, we have seen events such as the #MeToo movement and #BlackLivesMatter sweep across the world. In Australia, the Marriage Act was changed in December 2017 to allow persons of the same sex to marry, and climate changes resulted in bushfires on a scale never encountered before in summer 2019–20. Now the world is enduring a pandemic. Throughout these quite remarkable times, we have published women's voices from every continent except Antarctica and South America. Women have responded to the times and given our readers a unique insight into their lives. And I am delighted to say *Not Very Quiet* has lasted longer than Donald Trump's presidency. I thank the amazing network of women poets who have supported *Not Very Quiet* over these four years and eight issues. Special thanks to our very generous Guest Editors: Anita Patel, Lisa Brockwell, Kerrie Nelson, Tricia Dearborn and Anne Casey. Thank you to Sandra Renew, my co-founding editor, and to Tikka Wilson, our production manager. And a very special thank you to local Canberra and ACT regional poets and those from the wider Australian community for their unfailing and generous support of the journal. —*Moya Pacey*

EXPOSURE

i.

White marks on a black page; a photographic negative of loss. It's the view from the back of a mirror; the scene staring back from inside the looking glass. She steps around the scorched blank shapes; the final traces of humanity left on physical spaces.

ii.

The flash of detonation has seared every nearby surface; the inverted shadows are all that remain of the people. On the Yorozuyo Bridge, they begin to tile over the silhouettes that still bear witness.

Cassandra Atherton

THIS AUTISTIC GUISE

may i stim before you, love? or
must i keep up with my masking? just

asking—should i solely seek to blend? conceal
my fingers' fairy flits, my mouth's capacious grin?

or will you see me wholly, love? in my most stimulated
form? uncamouflaged in rawness and wildly unadorned?

when i strip down to straightforward skin, could i cast
this guise aside? or would you rather i perform for

you? keep my tides in hide? play up that
faux allistic she i make-believe to be?

or would you see me unimpeded,
love? see me in my free.

Oakley Ayden

RHYTHMIC OSCILLATIONS

There is still light
already diluted
one last morning

you told me
head tilted towards the ground
that I had no sense of space
or maybe that was my own confession.

I might have been jaywalking
across a Sydney street
counting breaths against a backdrop
of honking cars
oblivious.

I breathe out
breath condenses
sound disperses into air
heat into dust.

You sing and there is no song
chords become the body
the body spins
the spin is atoms

time, of course, is up
that's not news to anyone
I try to be sad, but all I feel
is desire, kiss the ground
lie down and roll
like our dog after it has been washed
cover myself in loose dirt
the sheer luxury of it
coarse against my skin.

Lying here, in imaginary bliss
I know what we're losing
the price of failure

it's too much, too little
there is only now

sky-blue, stone-blue
sapphire, indigo
heartbreaking blue
the Earth breathes out.

Magdalena Ball

THE CAMEL AND THE STRAW

When there's nothing left to say you eat
knock back the red wine you ordered
begin the cigars I hate.

My mouth is full with all that you said
and I'm too damned polite to do the napkin thing
spit out the one line I can't swallow.

So I smile
no teeth
while inside I pack up and leave you.

J V Birch

MILLENNIUM

Remember when 1995 was shiny and new
everything unknown: five years before the millennium—
the magic year approaching fast, the one we'd all written
about in grade school: we'd ride hovercrafts to the mall and
we'd return the planet to full eco-balance complete
with restored forests and sleek modern buildings powered by
scent-less human excrement; toilets flush recycled water;
trash compressed into water resistant bookless libraries:
landfills eradicated while convenience multiplied.
When the odometer flipped 1996, 19-
97, 1998, closer to the magic
two and three zeroes, some still thought we'd flip to perfection
but many of us upon seeing the lack of unwheeled
levitating transport believed indicators pointed
to annihilation. Softly, softly, 1999
laughed at our canned food stacks, our computer backups and stored
hard drives, printed emails, bracing for the symbolic click
of the millennium. Quietly, 1999
tossed the storeroom key over with a stifled laugh.
The Gregorian calendar had no year zero.
The next day, once the champagne wore off and computers pinged
on bright as ever, we understood the joke, and ordered
another shipment of freeze-dried food for the next crisis.

Wendy BooydeGraaff

OUT WEST

Out west
tough, spiny *kwongan* blankets the ground
every winter
rainfall trickles through cracks in rocks
fills aquifers
and flowers bloom into a patchwork quilt
hiding honey possums and salamander fish
in the strange rainforest

seeing their opportunity
the white men in bulldozers razed the scrub
and
surprised
the roots gave way to bare sand

a great inland beach

but
out west
the rains come every winter
so they sprinkle fertilizer on the sand
drill wheat into the desert
plant vines
and wait for the breadbasket to grow
as men get drunk off the wine

the great aerial ocean
heaves
for lack of ozone
drawing the clouds down south
closer to the pole
and
the rain stops visiting like it used to

out west
once too wet dairy country
gives way to wheat fields
and wheat fields

watch the sunset on the Indian Ocean

there's nowhere left to grow to

salt creeps up through soil
glitters like a moonscape on top of rocks
the creeks run with it

tap water tastes like children drinking from the garden hose
left baking in the sun all day

out west
there'll be nothing left to farm
but dead stalks
and sand
and salt

and sand

and salt.

Emily Bourke

OUT IN THE OPEN

I've seen a lion throw his head back and roar to ensure maximum amplification
The lionesses mainly concern themselves with the silent skill of hunting, to ensure the survival of all.
But in 1991, a black girl in a white tracksuit
stood in a sports arena
And didn't pussyfoot around those high notes
that are hard to reach
It was like she was unleashing a torrent of energy,
like a bright fountain of song.
You could see the muscles in her out-thrust neck. There's so much more power where that came from.
And again, just last week, a young girl with her hair braided in a coronet flecked with gold; and a coat
colored like the sun itself
Poured cleansing words into the public space, to purify the contested place
Where small proud boys had created
A shambles: bringing shame down on themselves in front of their own ancestors and their own race.

It's unmasked, now: what breeds about the heart, the ugly beliefs under the 'be best' slogans and the ordinary amities of the fearful disinherited. Those lovely ladies making home made jam; these corporate warriors, now retired; their husbands all deciding who was overrunning the land, and who should not be seen or heard, or take up a position which can legitimately be admired.

Poets discuss the young sun queen, whose words lit a pyre and also carried forward a torch. CNN released a transcript afflicted with errors, so it was difficult to decipher the true meaning from the words themselves.

There was an image of an upward climb, through hardship to a desired summit—and no need for rappelling, because the climb was in the mind and the upbuilding sequences of the words. Serrated, and serried, each part igniting flares to light the way for the next. Each word, briefly unmasked, was robed in its own vivid, solid colour, and gloved in an elegance befitting winter.

The colours were on the inside too; woven in with the content of their character. Such a solace, after so many years of hollow surface.

Burnished women, brazen with ambition,
embodiments of aspiration. But it is the work
done in the quiet of night, alone, sifting
through the not so good thoughts and words

thrown at them as children

that make these public spectacles more than
what meets the eye.

Devika Brendon

THE ART OF COSTUME

In the christening scene of Sleeping Beauty, the most joyful fairy wears bright pink. It's a costume her mother has made with a satin bodice, four layers of tulle and matching bloomers. That's how it really happens in 1961 at the Saint Brendan's Parish school hall.

This particular fairy has never played such an important role. Her rag-rolled ringlets bounce when her jiffies skim across the wooden floor. Organza wings aflutter, she hovers for a moment in the air, before tiptoeing towards centre stage where the baby princess is sleeping in a golden crib.

Beaming towards her audience she calls 'I GIVE HER JOY', in her loudest voice, all the while flourishing her wand. When she twirls sparks of joy whizz from its silver tip and spill across the audience. In this moment she discovers the reason for her existence so she twirls, and twirls, and twirls, filling every corner of the room with joy, until another whimsical fairy shoos her away.

watching
her mother apply lipstick
without a mirror
she perfects by heart
the art of painting smiles

Michelle Brock

WAITING ON IMRAN KHAN

I knew they were trouble the moment they walked in.
I was eighteen, bookish, I'd not yet learned
to build a public face. I was laid open like an oyster
on a salted plate. The uniform was no help,
nylon trousers cut into my soft waist and thighs,
standard issue, there was no bigger size. Summer—the dozy

lunch time shift. Office workers, pensioner couples
sharing, before the cool waterhole of the cinema.
Then, eight or nine men all preening, careening,
igniting against each other. Who was the roughest,
who had the biggest, who was alpha,
and who was his bitch. With my greeting (guinea pig

tentative, I kick myself now), I became the pitch
for a practice hit; a boy's own way to rejig
the middle order of the Pakistani cricket team.
I'd never admired Imran Khan as a cricketer—
too cool and vain—I preferred flashy and passionate
like Dennis Lillee, or stately and dignified

like Clive Lloyd, but even so, it should have been
a thrill. I'd been following the Test series,
a fan since Dad and I sat on The Hill.
For a young man they might have been jovial,
but when I seated them they broke into a dirty laugh,
staring hard at parts of me. I delivered their tray of Pepsi,

my hands shaking so the glasses sang like bells;
not one of them took pity. Imran Khan sat
at the centre. He said something I did not understand
and some of them hooted, one snarled, their eyes
were hot monsters, some swearing softly,
gesturing at me. I met his eye for a long moment

and saw carefully manicured disgust
at the humiliation I was heaping upon myself
by being a young woman, by walking the floor

in my awful uniform, my flat, black lace-up shoes. Yes,
I was walking the floor: earning my own money, slowly
forming the dense quartz of my opinions, polished and patient.

Lisa Brockwell

THE FEMINIST

At the party
when I said
I was a feminist

All the men
left the room
clutching their cans of beer.

They returned
and huddled
in another corner.

I continued
debating
on safer things

The terrorist threat
social justice
the refugee crisis.

The men returned
offering me glasses
of wine

And an
opportunity
to dance.

Denise Burton

MALTHUS

Swigging from her over-sized sea-blue water flask, she never noticed the fish that slid into her. She mistook its dance for the quickening and stocked up on Clear Blue pregnancy tests. Squatting over the red bucket she emptied herself, threw the sticks in and stirred the jetsam with a wooden spoon. After three minutes she fished them out patting each along the edge of the fringed beach towel. A fin, a gill, a cold rimmed eye. She arranged the small windows, piecing together the cerulean lines. Sometimes, results can be consequence.

Monica Carroll

IN ONE HUNDRED DAYS

An old man
scrawls his name
and smiles.

The earth
travels two hundred and fifty-seven million kilometres;
three hundred billion stars go dark.

A tiny cluster of cells
evolves into a fifteen-kilo baby polar bear;
one hundred and thirty-seven cubic kilometres of antarctic ice-caps melt.

A royal empress tree
stretches four and a half metres higher;
two thousand four hundred animal species die out

My sons grow two centimetres taller;
almost one million children perish from hunger;
an eight-year-old American girl is killed by a US airstrike.

An old man scrawls his name
seventy-nine times
and smiles.

Anne Casey

I WILL FALL SICK IF YOU PHOTOGRAPH ME

26 December 2004

Infinite decay at the shores of the Andamans.
Rumour of apocalypse on streets heavy

with the marrow of civilization;
caught in time's suck and blow.

Bones on boats/on trees/on windows/
on the collapsed lips of the earth.

Except them.

They who gathered the mist of moon fall,
cared to speak to the brindled turtle,

mapped the gloomy haze over hushed waterways,
released tremulous bird calls from their palms.

They rose at the edge of the deluge,
swooned to the wild beats of the dawn

and bribed no expensive gods
to break into a blossom.

Then came the sentinels of culture
to write on the stunned tongues of technology,

'the tribes are alive'.
A triumphant answer to 'man's search for man'.

But to the lust of their lenses,
said the finite forest child, 'I will fall sick if you photograph me'.

He did not wish to become a shadow in the wind
or the last wave in the 'age of rising seas'.

With a bow and arrow on his ash-smeared shoulders,
he departed—One last sea-lion gaze at the mossy black of the night,

slow and humming into the woody hollows,
perhaps a prayer for rain:

for everyone to drink a little
for everyone to bathe a little

Jhilam Chattaraj

CHEONGSAM

Costume and custom are complex.
'Exchanging Hats', Elizabeth Bishop

At the bottom of my wardrobe: eight dresses,
tailor-made for me. It was me who scoured

the fabric shops, who unwound each bolt
so flowers spilled across the floor like spring.

I was the one who picked out each set
of frog buttons, matching roses to roses,

butterflies to wing. The seamstress bound each edge
in contrast silk piping. I eschewed the traditional

fastenings, requesting instead a hidden back zip
so I could singularly dress and undress myself,

stepping in and out of my costume with sleek ease.
She had saved fabric at the seams for the inevitable

spread of womanhood that would come with marriage
and children. Slits just long enough for a girl

to take small steps; forcing her to sit, knees together,
revealing only a length of leg to the watching men.

The higher the collar, I used to think, *the more elegant*
the wearer. So tight I couldn't speak. The lady

who sewed my cheongsam died several years ago.
The woman who wore those dresses? She climbs

in shorts, she struts in trousers, she dances in skirts;
she is wholly clothed and naked in her own bright skin.

Eileen Chong

MOST DEADLY

We glow light deadly.
We be see-thru blue-bell floating
Laugh at your thick meat hang kicks
Tend tenderly to our tentacles. Ribbon beauties
That slap death like crack whips.
If you come here you play by fathom deep rules.
Your pounding blood heart weigh down
Strung out nervy system so puzzle scared of we.
Venom is survival down here. Stay out of our
Tangle way. Is that so hard? You who build
Carapace in multiples to carry all you scuttling
Greed across the seas.
You who cling desperate to thinking you are Gods.
You need us. Breath-take terror hungry gaze: *look
How they move like magic*. Ethereal murderers stuff of
Your nightmares we tap at your bulbous brain
Dumb mouthed hubris. We will not be boxed
By your jelly name for we.
Watch us translucent pulsing tendril dance.
Be awed. Gape. Jaw struck.
We whisper slip into your dreams to prod:
'You are not everything you are not even most things.'
Shiver mortal face raised hands clasp
Gratitude. At us mystery.

Emilie Collyer

TRICKS OF THE TRADE

The Playwright, In The First Week Of Rehearsal, Makes Herself Plain

'She has beautiful shoulders,' I said. 'And the light pours off of her skin.'

Because an actor can do anything she took a breath and shone. But then

all the female actors who had been listening in had beautiful shoulders

and light pouring off of their skin. I had to rein them in. There was too

much light bouncing around the rehearsal room. 'No,' I said. 'Just her.'

I know too much about this game but I don't know everything. Outside

the homeless squatted, in distressed costumes, smoking bumpers, waiting

in a ragged line for the free lunch. Hunkered deep into their roles. An apt

tableau. 'Perfect, perfect,' whispered the playwright. 'Don't change

a thing.' We could smell the free lunch cooking as we clattered back from

bistros. The downcast eyes took in our feet, but one or two lifted a glance

with a curious squint, a cool and tilted assessment of the portion we would get. Then we were gone, one blink, we were no longer there, we were voices

ringing from inside the old church hall, emphatic footsteps dancing to my tune.

Jennifer Compton

THE DUSKY GRASSWREN

(Amytornis purnelli)

They live in spinifex
sharp as needles.
Slips of twitchable feather
avoid piercing
by miraculous instinct.

Piping shrilly,
higher than some can hear,
they pop up.
The Scottish word *wee*
is all I can think of.

Cats relish them,
but the spinifex,
sharp as cats' claws,
gives them
almost a chance.

They lurk,
way below the parrots
who flaunt and flap.
Grant that such tiny brown
still finds islands of spike.

PS Cottier

GETTING IN THE WAY and SCIENCE

GETTING IN THE WAY

Intending to chop wood he chopped the bad girl in half. People didn't like this but the bad girl got in the way. She got in the way of the man and in the way of the axe and in the way of the wood and in the way of the job. Finally, she got in the way of keeping warm and making soup because she didn't burn well. People didn't care about any of this but they cared a lot about punishment. They said, 'You are a bad man' but they did not consider what that might mean he would get in the way of.

SCIENCE

We must determine if the lovers are as they say. We know they act like fractals. We know they feel gravity. Would they use a horse-whip on each other though? And is it possible to find out how they came into being and if, in fact, they're an invariant set?

MTC Cronin

INTERIOR WITH WARDROBE MIRROR

After the painting by Grace Cossington Smith

How civilized in 1955
to have a full-length mirror
so I can turn my back
and stretch my neck around
just so, to check my stocking
seams are straight.
No self-respecting soul
would venture out
with wobbly ones, except
perhaps my paternal aunts
who wouldn't dare go
anywhere without hats, gloves
and stockings. There they are
today in summer heat, holding
hands as they peer into shop windows
thinking all is well with the world.
How could I break their spell?
No, I cannot tell them ladders
are the order of their day
and pantyhose now holds sway.

Jan Dean

SCAR MASSAGE

a tiny section of my body
was excised, sent off for biopsy

a day or two later
somebody jokingly asked
how I thought my mole was going

I found I could not bear to think of
that small piece of me
floating in clear fluid in a plastic bottle
in a pathologist's office

irretrievable, irrevocably
exiled

I was left with a cavity
that has sealed itself over
with the help of two continuous sutures

now that the stitches are out and a week has gone by
I massage the scar for five minutes twice a day
using, as advised, two fingers
and as much pressure as I can tolerate
to prevent the join
hardening

I am astounded by the depth of its colour

other parts of me have been lost
other scars left to harden

these are not so visible

I have stopped ignoring them nonetheless
have stopped trying to disguise them
with complaisance, competence, facts-at-the-ready

I return to them, feel for
their shapes under the surface
attest their presence
with as much pressure as I can tolerate

I speak to them

tell them
that they are no longer alone

Tricia Dearborn

ON JOY HESTER'S LATE PORTRAITS OF GIRLS

Sun behind her on threadbare floor,
at thirty-seven, draw
girl and dog in ink,
a yearning, younger self
has dabs of nail polish pink,
girl and gold-washed hound,
peaceful on the (h)earth,
'gainst the ground of brown.

And did dogged drawing of
Girl with Dog,
Girl with Goanna,
Girl with Hat and Far Away and
Girl with a comet tail,
dull the burn of radiotherapy?

Those *Girl* portraits
hung stark in the winter dark
and shuttered at Heide
from your view
through cigarette smoke and the
hubbub of Hester's lovers and contemporaries
now streaming into the gallery
from the Field of Reeds.

Sally Denshire

BLACK DREAM BIRD

It was yesterday
that I was a crow
with horse hair in my beak
and my nest half built
and my black feathers
shining through the early mist
of belonging to the world
of knowing how to balance
on the air of the world
and my shadow
the same colour as myself.

Even when the farmer
tied my body lifeless
to the wire in warning
and my bones poked out
still I flapped in the wind
and raised my wings
my beak hinged open
to the call of the air.

Moyra Donaldson

OUR DAILY TREAD

a five kilometre loop of beaded observations
gate-path-road-park-wetlands-storm water drain

a rosary performed with feet
each inhalation guarded by a mask as seasons turn

now walking is our new religion
a warrant to the great out-through-the-doors

lockdown escape fuelled by $1 Servo coffee
at the first station of the cross

late summer shade falling to slip-hazard leaves
acorns, nuts and conkers booby-trapping the way

the spiky fruit of the towering plane trees
Covid-19 made manifest

as collectively we plough a new desire path
1.5 metres from the cement

thus we can pass on a held breath
exhale into cloth at the bridge to the other side

Jane Downing

A FEAST OF A WARDROBE

I met a girl who was in the business of eating
clothes. She said she was tired of wearing them,

and the talk of other girls wearing them or not
wearing them. It sounded like a market bound to

succeed in our *socioculturalenvironmentalpolitical*
landscape and so I asked her, how do you do it. Oh,

it's simple, she said. You rip this seam here. Just
pull the pieces apart like that. You can use kitchen

scissors if you like, anything at all. Loose threads
add texture, so don't worry about removing them.

And then, she said, you just put it in your mouth,
and you chew.

I joined her for dinner that night. She worked her
way through two pairs of ripped jeans and a lacy

bra. I ate the pair of shorts I'd worn when I was
eleven and Joshua Gordan had grabbed me by

the ass. The denim stuck in my throat like it had
teeth of its own. Does this get easier, I asked her.

Oh no, she said, not at all. So why do you do it, I
said. Well, a girl's got to process this shit somehow,

she told me. Besides, I take 'you are what you eat'
very seriously—one day I'm sure *whoiam* will

match *whattheysee*. She smiled: there were bright
blue threads in her teeth. I shoved another length

of fabric into my mouth. And another. And another.
And another. It's about bloody time they made a

banquet fit for a queen, I said, and brandished a metal button in the air. Stuff this in the eye of the

beholder.

Natasha Dust

THE STRONGEST GIRL IN THE WORLD

'So. How do you trim ya pubes?'
She was sparkling, I was mumbling, stopped thick
as I realised that this boy I picked had told,
told them all, in this shocked hard heart-beat teenage lunch—
'I dunno,' I said. 'I don't do much.'
'Still,' she smiled. 'You wanna give 'em a bit of a trim.'
(And my throat sealed up as the walls roared in.)

When I was four I had a hero.
She was the
STRONGEST GIRL IN THE WORLD!
PIPPI LONGSTOCKING, vaulting the gable-pole,
long brown legs
like a wheeling shot of hot kinetic energy she
hurled policemen up through the sky, and with a
bright 'So long!' she
flung the bullies face down in the shrubbery.
Four years old, she drove me wild—I went crazy,
jumping up and down in front of the TV: Pippi! Who,
with a running jump sailed over the cliff—
plunked down, without a scratch—
because she couldn't conceive she'd be hurt
had not once launched
a chastened trajectory.

And it was Pippi
who moved in me then, worlds later
in the teenage dark
strangely detached and half-afraid
but in the centre
of that cool, still calm SHE stirred: a flame.
I was virgin, fearless, hairy like a little wolf
My innocence didn't pull me back but
pushed me, moved
not by affection, or
by attraction, but:

    because I was brave.

I think of little girls. I wonder who they're watching.
My little cousin, she loves
MERIDA: who rips off the hood to reveal her bristling hair, she loves
PONYO: alive, defiant, striving, right
to the top of the wave.
I can only hope they're with her,
when she's old enough to make that jump.
When she has to brace her back
in the face of cruel humiliation,
when her time comes
to heave off the titan weight of shame.
When she has to be
the STRONGEST GIRL IN THE WORLD—
I hope
she turns out brave.

Eugenie Edquist

SPRING PURPLES WITH COAST TEA TREE AND GOLDEN WATTLE

with Paulownia tomentosa, Leptospermum laevigatum and Acacia pycnantha

Its genus named for majesty, this backyard tree spills
lilac. Rainbows rush bright to tongue nectar in its

blossoming. Being is choral. A chrysalis of days is
contingent on code that bounces onscreen. The ABC

backdrop matches the news presenter's tie. Magenta.
Wattle purpose is golden drift beside a creek, where

tea trees petal soft on path. A crush of coastal
befalling. Avoidantly, masks flower. Online we've

learnt—that this novel thing will thrive, will escape
our best intent, will break apart with   lather.

Anne Elvey

IN HALF LIGHT

On Margaret Olley's Dressing table (self portrait), 1982

The tilt of an old-fashioned
mirror-on-a-stand finds her.
On that carved platform

artefacts of contemplation,
the glass vessels of beauty,
become a luminous threshold

guarding her bereaved self.
Her dream gaze looks inward
and, at a sideways angle, outward.

The iris of her left eye
holds a catchlight
like a misshapen tear.

Set against the mirror,
a mask-image, lids steeply closed
in meditation, or death,

takes shape from arctic blue,
teal, and the chrome green
so loved by the artist.

Those same colours abide in
the wallpaper's summer leaves
winding across backlit lapis—

sumptuous, yet end-of-day sombre:
    the blue of mortality,
    the blue of immortality.

Daylight fans in, leaving
half her face in shadow while
enfolding these chosen things,

precious or plain,
which speak the inspiration of
Chardin, of Morandi—

who laboured freely, exactly,
devotees of the numinous lure
of the inanimate.

Her musing self,
eye to eye with its double,
drinks, sip by sip,

a draught of truth
as the room, and the world,
fade, bloom.

Diane Fahey

AT LEAST I STILL REMEMBER

there was never
any doubt of love
in my childhood
dahlias grown by dad
vibrant in mum's vases

~

Empire Day:
my father in the garden
lighting fireworks
while I watched, enthralled
behind the kitchen window

~

bias binding
one of those dread items
clever mother
wielded when teaching
her dull daughter to sew

~

Grandma
crocheted most beautifully
round the edges
of our linen hankies …
all gone now, every one

~

too late to know
it was always you
from the start …
still, I can cherish
those Elvis recollections

Amelia Fielden

MASQUE

this. this mascara-blacked dark. it closes on you. blue-blank light refracts. split maniac. slit open in the shadows, sliding from your pale pall. half-light, half-life. apple flesh lies, going sweet sick. an affirmation of a heart, a piece of muscle writhing uneasily, instinctively. words come easily to you. they were put into your head by a kindly hand. stone golem. so you seem. so you will yourself to be. often, your talk is cheap as candles, waxen and senseless, leaving that burnt odour. when the wicks blacken, slacken, silence reels out. oil on water. your appearance a blur of conviviality, lightly bestowed. swiftly slipping through lives with half-answered questions, half-truths. this death mask that you wear in life is clean and cold. the damp liquidity of setting plaster of paris, cracking with movement. you are a plague doctor, black beaked. lunettes de soleil catching at the light. dark mirrors, no answers. untouchable, walls within walls. your carapace of privacy, holding the distance with the authority of a god. the soul lines are strict, the paper-cut words clean, precise, numb. yet often, your leonard cohen eyes, wrong colour, right gaze, unloose from your bell jar. blurring, slurring the bounds of your apparent intention, they trespass. magnetised, electrifyingly direct, your pupils betray. under your denial, the tarmac swallows bell-hollow, sun-laden, foot-heavy. lampposts watch disbelievingly down the street. skin statue-paled, slightly razor-burned, with that dostoyevsky glitter in your eyes, you close your bruised lids. inside, crystalline forms foam out of the dark. for a moment, something shifts. niveous bulbs mouth the oily air. chiaroscuro, the night is of your colour. the fine weave of the ashen winding sheet is drawn back, unmasking everything.

Ellie Fisher

SELF-PORTRAIT IN THE BATHTUB

After Frida Kahlo's, What the Water Gave Her

Hers was a wash with water
of a certain shade, telling
this portrait
after the fact
mine is now a bloodless scene
a wash with no colour at all
signifying the lack.
If I hold my breath
it could be a ghost story
zooming in
on the murky ripples.

It is the silence
the feet out of water
that chills in those movies
the slow creep
of water circling.

The director knows
the power of stark white tiles
negative spaces, outlines, shadows
the terror of the unspoken shade
nothing to see here, now
no telling Daliesque reenactments
just the same foreboding drain
just feet
disembodied.
Bloodless.

Anna Forsyth

POINTILLISM WORKSHOP AT GOOTCHIE, 1976

Let's go and get drunk on light again—it has the power to console. Georges Seurat

Home…Tiaro…Bauple Mountain…Gootchie
We followed the dots

In the Fairmont. Artists emerged like sprites
from among the gums

You were bronze-skinned and smiled when
I said there was a frog in the loo

I had a small table next to yours, dappled cows
brown and dogs white

You retaped my paper again and again,
said I was a true *artiste*

We ate corned beef sandwiches wrapped in foil,
tried damper off hot coals

You stood in the shed doorway, sun surfing
corrugations in your hair

And used a fat brush (for hours it seemed)
to daub on the green mountain

You swore a bit when you weren't sure
if it looked right and then

We drank red cordial from the esky while
that layer dried

You took a fine brush to speckle over ghost
trunks in white bands,

Their shadows dolloped indigo and pink,
sky: yellow, mauve and tan

So the mixing happened with your eyes
not on the palette

And as we drove away, I could still see the
Gootchie bush artists

Through thick dirt, splattered red, little
points of light waving

Jane Frank

WOMAN QUITS FEMININITY

She is hanging up her mask,
colourful as it is,
they say 'easy on the eye'.
Let the glances fall where they may,
they won't touch her.

She is taking off her heels.
No, they won't make her
reach the stars, no more
tiptoeing through life.
Time to put her foot down,
stand *her* ground.

She is throwing out her razor,
it's no longer appealing
to throw out time and money. Instead
she will sharpen her tongue
to cut off opinions not called for.

She is stepping off the scales—
they can't measure up to her.
She will feed her hunger,
no need to deny herself
humanity.

Irina Frolova

ALL THE WILLING HOURS

> *& we shall walk & talk in gardens all misty with rain*
> *& never never grow so old again*
> Inscription, Wendy Whiteley's Garden, Sydney

Narrow paths centre the terraces through
fig and flame and bangalow palm; leaves jostle

the storeys with shape and shade and tint
any leaf will take. A sanctuary with roots

in her childhood; Lavender Bay her own
rampant alchemy to wander in, like a painting.

And for us too, picnic tables, a bell hanging
in meditation, a birdbath from a cast-out sink.

With her hair wrapped in folds of iris-blue, Wendy
talks of how she replaced the debris among

the coral trees, cutting by cutting, plant
by plant and mulch, to revere them here:

her lover, their daughter. How all the willing
hours bloom unexpected grace from loss.

Kathryn Fry

CHRISTMAS IN NOVEMBER 2019

At the end of our first was, of course, a second and, yes,
a third glass of wine.

And some time into the second was a badly built joint,
made from my paper, your cardboard, my tobacco, your bud,
my spit, all passed from your free hand to mine.

We had to go around to the bins. You were wrapped
in tinsel, I had antlers, the joint sitting between my teeth. My
lighter, your fingers, my breath, your breath. We left the lighter
on the park bench, forgot about the wine, carried home only
ourselves.

    And I thought,

Even if this is not the end of history, even if you are to move or I am to cheat or
we are never to be anything of note—In years coming, I will still have this piece of
tinsel in my collarbone, this wine in my belly, this piece of rolling paper stuck on
my bottom lip.

Sophie Furlong Tighe

PANDORA'S KITCHEN

Epimetheus shuffled Pandora
into the house
with slight trepidation;
her skin still seemed too soft,
too new.

Here is the bed.
Here is the grain.
Here is where we build the fire.

Pandora tiptoed into the kitchen,
trailed her fingertips along the counter
and over the stacks of unwashed dishes
while Epimetheus watched, giddy
as a bottle of champagne.

Here is where you pluck the chickens like lyres.
Here is where you bake the daily bread.
Here is where we fill our bellies
with all the goodness from your oven.

Pandora felt his eyes dig into her
like twin sickles. Felt her flesh
grow red. Turning away, her errant
elbow sends the water jug crashing to the floor.

The familiar curves reduced
to shards at her feet.

Pandora stared at the ruined thing,
then at her husband, then back down
and began to scream.

Allison Goldstein

NOH

After Walter de la Mare

Slowly, silently, masked like moons,
they walk the night in tabi shoes.
Across the bridge from the divine,
stories threaded in the pine
that stands for ever at the back
of centre stage as spotlights catch
men who kneel in neat culottes
and strike the music's paradox.
Awakening the ghosts still deep
in ancient lands' mysterious sleep;
released from history, gliding by,
visors hiding silver eyes,
assuming that we too have been
drifting down their silver stream.

Hazel Hall

EATING THE REEF

Solomon Islands, Uepi

Adrift, pursuing phantoms of lost habitats
we pursue wilderness until it is no more.

I am eating the reef.
At first, it is sweet and expansive—

like meditation, or the rush of oxygen
after holding the breath.

Ocean so blue it is sky and sea at once—
cobalt blues gas the coppers

of midnight snapper,
following courses electric

of bluefin trevally and barracuda;
we submerge and are joyfully lost.

Powder fire of faecal matter
scatters down like talcum

as fish accelerate
and weave the ocean's current

that silts glorious accretions
of sucker-mouthed worms and corals.

I hang trawler nets of grief and avarice
and fill them with fish.

Quartets of seniors float
in the channel's shallows like plastic

bottles eddying the pier.
Masks full, they stand and crunch coral—

the newly buoyant flail.
Deeper out, I float

the surfaces of black tip reef sharks
and wish for blood,

or for the lips of giant clams
to swallow us whole.

Kristin Hannaford

WANTED—PRINCESS

Well established Prince

    seeks energetic

Princess to run busy castle.
The qualified applicant must
be a multi-tasker proficient

    in financial management

animal husbandry

    as well as the more mundane

aspects of day-to-day

    household management.

The successful candidate will have
child bearing abilities

    as well as maintaining

top-rank beauty

and ability to satisfy her Prince

    every night.

Knowledge of magic

    and diplomatic relations

with magical beings is a plus.
Please apply in person.

Position is expected to fill quickly.

Michelle Hartman

LETTER TO A BRIDE TO BE

Thank you for sharing with me the newest (yet quite retro) issue of *Vogue Bridal Patterns*. I love that off-white shot silk you brought back from your travels and think it would suit your complexion perfectly. It looks much better than the Nora white organza. It's also a tribute to your integrity and I hope I'm not reading too much into your choice of colour. But before you start making the dress, I urge you to indulge in a little intertextual journey around your maiden room, if I may say so, for I'm not sure you know on what *galère* you are embarking. Mark my words. I don't mean *gondola*, or anything romantic, but *galley*, a low, flat ship with one or more sails (glad you opted for a visor instead of a veil) and up to three banks of oars worked by slaves. First, as an artist, you must re-read Tennyson's 'The Lady of Shalott' against the grain. Then turn to Elizabeth Bishop's 'The Gentleman of Shalott' and Jessica Anderson's *Tirra Lirra by the River*. I studied both in year twelve (wish I'd paid more attention). Finally, and this may surprise you, especially coming from me, read Henrik Ibsen's *A Doll House*, a work your father drew on to devise our home. Deep down, I now think Ibsen understood the difference between need and desire; desire and love; love and lust. Your father would disagree, of course, but I would maintain that Ibsen was really a proto-feminist writer. Wink. One last thing: beware of identifications. With two (anti) heroines bearing your Christian name, you wouldn't want to become unduly hystericised. Much love. X

Dominique Hecq

THE SEA CALLS MY NAME

'Night swim in the sea baths'

*After James Drinkwater, oil on canvas,
2018, Newcastle Regional Gallery.*

the smell of salt
takes me back

I stand on the sea wall
trust the skin of the water
to part when I dive

I float
through my dreams
patterns and shards of light
swim through blue patches
reflected memory of day-sky

I am starfish, mermaid
angel fish, under
moon's silver triangles
I climb ladders of light

and when I find
a sea urchin sheared
of its punk hairdo

to a grey stippled shell

I remember
its line of defence
its crisscross of spears

the carapace it wore to survive

washed out by the tides
from mouth to anus
a gift from the sea

its dead self
tattooed with memory

as the past calls me
back to where I began

Gail Hennessy

WHERE WE GO

C'mon, let's go with our attention depending,
with the ardour of late afternoon's pink horizon,
its cloud tendril, bird scrawl, and our questing
attachments—'there is such beauty'—but
it's the 'such' that contains a caution about
our exhausted hair or souls or the still sanguine way
we negotiate September's impatient buds
along the terraces, and our way through
another discussion at a corner, all the busy figures with
swathed loads and tenacity, what choices—a stop/go giggle
or something serious about the quickening splendour
of the road, its corrugations shining, a place indeed
for a hungry soul, or at least destiny full of flare,
where wires hover, machines quiver as if they know
who really owned all of this here, it's not for you and me,
not even the late shit rolling across the path, plastic
shit with purpose—there was a cost, we missed it—
the tentacles of the program spiral from the mall,
from the phones, 'it all seems so smooth,' you say,
and what can I reply, what can I gesture at
that's not the same lie as memory, that's now in
the program, you say 'see, even the dresses
watch us, demand something from our bodies'
but I don't follow your eyes there, I take your hand,
'c'mon,' I want to say, we can hitch onto a vision
outside the city's halls, past the parks, the river curves,
past the future to somewhere a bit like this as if
it's actually intense, routine and baffling like that place
where we go everyday. C'mon, let's find such
beauty among our bodies and common splendour.

Jill Jones

HONGOEKA LOVE POEMS

Warning at dawn
from the carvers at the pou:
Mana atua
Mana whenua, Mana
tangata: pay attention.

*

Midday, low-tide dive.
Water clear and mind-numbing.
Snakestail star, brittlestar, Cook's
Turban. Like the man himself
I shouldn't be here.

*

Well, I was invited,
even if I'm unworthy
of the gift and hardly know
the rules. I'm paying this debt
with Hongoeka love poems.

*

Disturbance on the
water. I wade past the reef
towards the boil-up.
Tiny fins track the surface:
dog sharks, learning how to hunt.

*

Steering wheel molten
in the late summer sun.
Slip through the marae
gates: Hongoeka Bay like
platinum. Like time-travel.

*

Drawn-out afternoons.
Lawns gone brown without winter.
Whiskey in one hand

weeder in the other
you're digging out dandelions.

*

Pōhutukawa
glows in the heart at sunset.
Sun alive, like us.
Red filaments on water.
High tide at Hongoeka.

*

Moon at three-quarters.
Blood dust on the beach's lip.
Silver shawl draws up
Rangituhi's shoulder. I
stand completely still.

Michaela Keeble

OH! SO DELICIOUSLY

her blue jug
astride the breakfast table
loose lipped
handle on hips
all the things he said
she should never be

too round
for shadows to loiter
too blue
for clouds to drift through
too patterned and far far
too *everything* ... yet

not slender
enough nor elegantly
resplendent
just plain and under-fired
where glaze doesn't shine
the way he wants her to be

her blue jug
the one she reaches for
to pour cream
over snap-crackle-pop
or whatever however
wherever she is

enough to make her
poetically
sweetened
unrepentantly
playful
and oh! so deliciously real

Kathy Kituai

FLORA CLOTH

Your dress looks like candied wheat.

Small tulips drip from your ears.

I can't praise your ears enough. Freckled and soft,

containing a solar system of hearing me.

You seem like the weekend.

You seem like gleaming grain.

I adjust my face to reflect you better.

To hold your mastery of involvement.

The oats are caramel, are spreading. The table

of new, hot pancakes and blueberry syrup.

We lay low in this young room. I'm acting

casual, making it difficult for anyone

to have me. I've seen you

turning. The will's in the harvest.

The strawberry air goes sour in its own excitement.

Kimberly Lambright

X300

On stage aerial legs sprout splayed feet. Skin-linked to land-sun-sky
dancers slide under, over and through each other's curves and caves.

    It's Jive Time in the fifties
    and the Mother Fucker Country
    wants space to quietly detonate a bomb.
    The Cold War's clouding an atmosphere
    so yellow the stuff's puffed up in the desert
    where no-one lives so no harm's done.

The smoke machine's in overdrive. We inhale it from the aisles.
Hunch down, crouch low to escape the pressing shroud

              but particles drift   from the plan to the plain

    shaken in a silent windstorm   settling over water holes and

        all that   breathes.

broken weeping ulcerated seeping
branded with cicatrix and radiation burns.

No-one's in the desert so no harm's done.

                                                    Robyn Lance

COMMUNION

Every instant, I just miss. The one who left the sachet twist at my café table and whose body heat remains in my seat. The one who stood, just here, smoking a still-vivid cigarette. The one who palped this pomegranate with five fingertips but replaced it in the ruddy pile, or left trace Chanel in this lift, like a clue, or last returned this library book, read or unread.

My mother frets at names mislaid: second cousins, book-club titles, the Minister for This or That. She is brightened when I remind that we are evolved for hearth-groups, not the metropolis—for acquaintances numbering fewer than a hundred, even fewer of them dear, a handful of books, to be read and re-read. Yet in my heart I am enraptured by the never met, the name never-shaped in my mouth, the heat in the seat, the book maybe read, and here on the ground, deposited an instant ago, a fragile cylinder of ash the size of a stranger's drawn breath.

Penelope Layland

FROM THE GARLIC WIFE

                    my parents honeymooned
in niagara falls. it's an old

story. our bedroom walls
                    stained with parliaments,
model planes, a tired

                    stamp collection
I found, years later,
                    in the kitchen drawer.

there were also pinking
                    shears, rosary beads,
a collection of unwanted

                    tradesmen, miracles
hourly, in neon, pulsing like the last
                    sun rise of a failing earth.

                    later, he moved
to a desert place, slicing
                    grapefruit in a new language

I married by the ocean
                    in a second-hand veil
astonished by the weight of my dress at the ceremony.

Nellie Le Beau

A GIRL DIES EACH NIGHT ON TV

Displayed like small paintings of horror.
Unearthed by bulldozers; revealed

from scrub, and ditches—
the face down nakedness of the form.

And something in us wants this.
A re-enactment on the night streets,

the men behind the cameras blowing
in their hands; the parked cars and

the lights, the storefronts
showing their bright interiors still open.

(To see the detective triumph
the girl must die first—the strong

female detective triumph. We stare
at her lips as she stares at the girl.)

Something in us needs to hear
the sound of footsteps; the CCTV

footage. To play her back then forward
to see her last moments, to wind her

and wind her. To wear her out.

Wes Lee

PLAYING DEAD

You've done what Nature expected of you
and all you want to do now is carry on.
Find a nice place to lay the eggs,
protected from predators and weather.
A sheltered, aqueous spot.

After that, you can dart around ponds,
or bask in the sun
where your forewings and hindwings
become stained glass. A curiosity
that children point at and admire.

When the headache excuse doesn't work
(because it doesn't in dragonflies)
what is she to do?

The dragonfly has to think fast.
Stalked mid-flight,
she falls into the undergrowth
to lie perfectly rigid
to avoid encounters with frisky suitors.

Then, free of them, she resurrects.
Wings glide freely through air
for on a sun-filled day
everything seems possible,
even a good night's sleep
in the secluded greenery.

Rosanna E. Licari

JUST BEFORE COVID-19 HITS I SELL MY GOLD

Three universes collide at the corner of Money and Monger streets in the centre of Perth. The moment we swing our feet from the car, the layers swirl for a moment like liquid amber leaves, then rustle to the ground: White Settlement over Whadjuk Noongar Boodja with a South-East-Asian Chinese influence. The narrow streets and shophouses remind me of Malaysian Chinatowns.

We walk towards the Cash and Gold Exchange. Sam Wagan Watson, my ghosts do not rise from the bitumen like O-rings of smoke, mine step out of Jimmy Tsui's kung-fu school on Monger St in Seven Star Praying Mantis fighting style. They are old, they are Chinese, and they are female, down to the last woman. They have dyed black permed hair, gold earrings and jade bangles, and they wear polyester pants with floral blouses. They line the sidewalk, holding their kung-fu poses. The only thing that moves is their reproachful eyes.

The world has changed, I hiss. *My life won't be like yours.* We push open the brown glass door. I lay them on the bench: the 24 carat Credit Suisse gold bar pendant, the star and heart charms link bracelet, the snake pattern bracelet. Wedding and engagement presents all. The Chinese businessman looks at me. He knows what they are. *It's been twenty-four years, and I never wear them*, I say. *I'm taking my youngest child to California and I want some spending money.* He nods as I sell my survival gold for tickets to Universal Studios.

> *wind curls down the street,*
>
> *rustling leaves as it goes,*
>
> *the stop sign—ignored.*

Miriam Wei Wei Lo

A SECRET MIDTOWN GARDEN

Our first apartment bordered ugly Hell's
Kitchen, a place for hanging your head out
The window, yelling for 'police, police!'

The back door was my savior, leading me
To jade insertions of a picket fence
That hid a missing piece of Paradise,
Green growing something quite unlike itself.

Here: rose aroma heavy in blue air,
Pink heliotrope lovely as a laugh,
Mature hydrangeas, honey in their cheeks,
Green eyefuls powering up two lives when
The wormy world of midtown leaves the mind
Without its moorings. Secret is our yard,
And lion-lit for us alone, as bold
As some unanswered prayers——survivor's way.

When he complains——'Always outdoors!' he'll say,
'Bent, knees-down!'——I plead debts I owe the day.

LindaAnn LoSchiavo

THE CRYSTAL MASKS OF LYNETTE AND DONALD

Lynette Wallworth stood up and spoke to the gathered elite in Davos.
Outside, the Swiss snow softened while at home ash rained
its sombre descent on the scorched earth (not yet official Government policy).
Lynette's voice, lucid, leaden in gravitas and intent,
did not cut through to the flat-earthers but only those who relished the shocks.
She's like crystal, thought Angela Merkel, *so deliciously shattering*.
Lynette, one of 100 leading global thinkers, wonders whether
the ephemera of thought will force the paradigm shift
the Prince of Wales implored with crystalline eloquence. *Such a pity
royal decrees are fossilised*, she thinks, *democracy is all well in theory
but to get anything done properly requires absolutism. Stop!
This thought cannot crystallise! Donald with life tenure?*
Instead, she creates a virtual reality of the new angel of death:
*We have seen the unfolding wings of climate change and we need
leaders for this moment.* She thinks of Greta (the girl was a natural),
and Uncle Nyarri who had never even heard a crystal radio
when the atomic blast was the spirit of his country that rose
up to speak while the water holes boiled and black mist
dotted the songlines through Maralinga, place of thunder.
Their voices will be heard now, thinks Lynette, *they are the leaders
for the new reality of black swans, tipping points and feedback loops.*
Donald notices that Lynette has not mentioned him. At. All.
He tweets *this Wallworth woman's opinion is worthless:
she is a perennial prophet of the apocalypse like Greta*. Besides,
his fortune teller's crystal ball has predicted that Ivanka
will succeed in 2024. *I am committed*, Donald tells the elite,
to conserving the majesty of God's creation.

Kate Lumley

WINGED AND KILLING AFTER CATULLUS

Some birds are hard to love
the blue heron
currawongs
wodjaloks with crimson wattles
growling from my balcony

        like dogs

I've seen one machete the soft neck
of a female in spring
then poke flimsy throats
of virgin grevillea
in a rhapsody of blood and foreplay

The driven
drop nerve agents on children
hurl acid in a woman's face

        on a Sydney Street

and that three-year-old washed up

        on the beach

his tucked-in shirt lifted
ever so gently by the ripple of an incoming tide
so he looked for a moment

        full of breath

                utterly alive

Julie Maclean

DISARMING

The girl is told that she is a bomb
at nine, or ten, or thirteen or when
men want to do what they want.
The girl is told that she is a bomb.
Her girl-bomb-body explosive, she makes the
men want to do what they want.
The girl is told that she is a bomb.
Her spark of existence will light the fuse
set explosion in motion beyond their restraint.
The girl is told that she is a bomb
that makes men say things, makes men do things,
makes men do things to her.
The girl is told that she is a bomb.
They gave her this power so that the men can
do what they want without consequence.
The girl is told that she is a bomb,
so it's just and right that she pays the price.
Look what she made them do!
The girl wishes that she was a bomb
whose eruption's destruction for men too close,
men who touch, men who are rough.

The girl is told she is not that kind of bomb.

The girl is told that she is a bomb
and must disarm and use her charm
so no-one gets hurt.

Jacqui Malins

TAKING A PICTURE

My grandmother's hands are a mosaic.

They've brought mango trees and gourds from Pakistan, planted them in the creases on her fingers. Sun-spots have woven themselves like patchwork on the back of her hand, camouflaging with generations of olive skin. Her veins have swollen since they fused her farm in Mirpur with her detached house in Lancashire. She tends to gaze at my father's nails to remember her own. They are, and always have been, coloured with the red henna she commands.

My grandmother rests her hand on mine, so I take a picture.

Sameeya Maqbool

ABRASION

blue seas, green islands—
the governance manipulator's dream of
paradise, the high ride on the wave
from grass to greenback on the tropic
cancer of poverty—
and in Australia the downers
(put them down and keep them down,
extract the juices from the ripened flesh
of the socially engineered to be exploited
and make them pay for the privilege)
spout fancy rhetoric
to the gullible about the betrayal
of democracy, about sanctions for sins
as if God alone, through the agency of his
corporate deputies, has given holy unction
to their own dis-graces;
and in Fiji
and Samoa and Tonga and the Solomons
the rich blue/green carpet of the Pacific
laid out under the throne of governance
where the coloniser sits, is wearing thin—
its patience threadbare; and once the strong
rough fibre of its weave is exposed it becomes
abrasive to walk on
with soft, white feet clad only
in the paper-thin currency
of words

Jennifer Kemarre Martiniello

BODHI OF A POEM

The good mother, when her belly swells,
listens to the moon.

From their granite beds
they can smell her intention,
so she digs secret nests at night,
and squats in violet shadows
to give birth.

The good mother holds her offspring
like a snowflake, tests its mettle
in the palm of one hand. A single drop,
yet to them it's more unsettling than a flood
or avalanche. They know how gravity works.
They know that even the littlest drip
can wriggle into nicks, splinter boulders,
invoke dust.

The good mother doesn't differentiate
between snow and stone,
she doesn't need to pick at the stitch
between gravel and its undoing.
The innovation of such a woman is muscular.
It has the guts to abseil expectations,
the nerve to carve a landscape
out of nothing but possibility.

The good mother dries her thighs.
They have forged a blade as sharp as any metaphor.
She knows they will cut her creation along its bias
and examine its entrails,
convinced they can predict what used to exist
between the words and silence.

Sometimes they patch it with catgut
before they cover it with a sheet.

Victoria McGrath

IN THE DUTCH TRADITION

when a person died, black cloth was draped
across all views to guard
the roaming soul from venturing outside.

She didn't hold with this idea.
So she chose one large picture: Connemara

on a good day, windless, treeless, grassy, dry,
a stretch of country she had never seen.
This graced the room she sat in going blind
for over twenty years, a mild sunlit scene

above the unlit space where her old head would rest.
The seeing soul … she thought its last
initiative should be to launch and fare
forward unencumbered into salt-bright air.

Kate Miller

BARTENDING

He came wanting attention; I lent him an ear
The customer's right though my salary's mine
He yearned for agreement—I gave it, I fear
Though he talked to my chest while I handed him wine

Thus he told me his tales of imagined offence
As I gave him a smile and then paid him no heed
For it's hard to engage with a tale that's pretence
Just another man wishing I'd plug up his need

Then his manner grew crass and I gave a small start
As his hand crossed the bench into room not his own
And he hissed snaking words he'd got down to an art
As he told what he'd do if I gave him a go

Yet I too have words I am willing to mention
If stuck at the bar with a man out of luck
For if I give one thing even less than attention
I fear it would have to be giving a f———.

Rosalind Moran

DIAPAUSE

An amber striped curve with shrieking back legs is blown on to my windscreen and there are so few of you Another bee buzzes around a window Flyspray too conveniently at hand I squirt Mistaken identity the blowflies awakened with the warmth I have often wondered if flies hibernate Not so Undergo diapause Like the more permanent state of insect parliamentarians

Lizz Murphy

REGENT THEATRES, EMPIRE HALLS

Our generation imitated what we saw
at matinees on Saturdays. In backyards
we dressed up like cowboys, Indians,
pretended to be every hero John Wayne
played, donned feather headdresses to star
as Crazy Horse or Pocahontas in battles
fought at Little Bighorn. We smoked
peace pipes, used groundsheets to make
tepees, built forts, conflated histories.
We knew of tribes called Cherokee,
Comanche, Sioux, and Navajo. Ignorant
of Australia's recent past, we had never
heard of Koori or Wiradjiri, but *Abo*,
had currency in our schoolyard.

In country towns in New South Wales
the Greeks ran cafes, the Poles made shoes,
the Germans rose to be more successful
than the landed gentry. Their children
went to school with us 'real Australians'.
A dark-skinned kid called Chocko said
he came from Pakistan. The Blackman
sisters reckoned they descended from
Kings and Queens in Tonga. Together
we learnt English history, paired up
and danced in Empire Halls. Puberty,
the '67 referendum, land rights demon-
strations, saw Chocko and the Blackman
girls remake history, build an Embassy.

K A Nelson

CAMILLE CLAUDEL

Your yearning. A weight
you birthed over
and over. You hauled

yourself through bronze,
from every version of exile
an arc

of limb, your hair
knotted with fury
and gleam. You were too savage

in your grace. Untamed,
too much a man in the colossal
precision of your hands.

How suddenly
they held nothing
but the white-air

of asylum. Fog heavy
as marble, still
as death.

Gemma Nethercote Way

AUGUST IN LAHORE

This thick heat swaggers
rolls its way over the canals, the bodies
of boys burned earth brown
glistening with sweat and water
as they dive among the refuse
clogging the city's waterways.

We cannot swim here, us college girls
in our cars and delicate clothes.
Not for us the raucous play
of boys who weave across the road
to their filthy oasis half naked
in the afternoon sun.

On the phone my father tells me
he used to play in the canals once
back when they were cleaner
and the sunshine less dusty.
He makes no wish for me
to do the same.

My starched muslins and lawns melt
into my skin and the days wrap
around me like wet sackcloth,
a dragging, dripping weight that air-
conditioning cannot lift. I think
of the boys moving in the dirty water
and wonder why staying dry feels
like drowning.

Nadia Niaz

ORDERLY QUEUE

we have forgotten history, world war two
footage of allied skeletal soldiers in rags
marching single-file, the brutal beatings, shouts
– or jewish citizens smuggled out of ghettos
escape long lines in concentration camps
taken to the sea, find asylum, settle, raise a family

six hundred thousand rohingya form a ragged queue on the skyline
cross the border, villages burn behind them, smoke clouds the sky
blood soaks the grass, they overflow tents on muddy ground

deals made with brutal regimes, a costly border force
stop the boats, those asylum seekers who did not drown
'jumped the queue' at sea, held hostage as deterrent
detained for years, kept prisoners in png
immigration minister's propaganda – 'had basically their own
personal butlers and cleaning maids up there'

hands on heads, men on manus form orderly queues, march to transit buses
pet dogs beaten to death or thrown from the bus window
refugees who fear violent locals with machetes, are arrested, handcuffed
some dragged kicking, beaten with long metal poles, forcibly moved
to a construction site, their futures undefined

jenni nixon

WATT AND THE ONION

Back in the days when they used to visit every year
before everyone got too old for it
my lad would say 'Do you know what?'
and his grandad would reply *'well yes
actually, I do. He was in my class at school.
Always had an onion in his pocket
which he'd ferret out, take a bite
and back in his pocket it would go.'*

Great Uncle John's Great Dane
used to wait stock-still, solemn-jowled
a trick shadow, pony sized
but with the wrong head
paying no mind to scraped knees,
wingnut ears, cowlicks, shouts and jeers
jumbling past over the other side of the wall,
eyes fixed only on bobbing school caps
just visible above the bricks
Gently, with purpose, he'd whip one off and trot away
chuffed with his prize.
Less gently, the lad wi' a bare head
would get a clip round the ear come home time.

Later, there were Woodbines and apple scrumping,
kick-the-can, near-drownings off Seaton Carew
where the offshore wind blew you past the pier
out into the foothills of the North Sea
ketchup sandwiches for tea and sometimes pease pudding
A good stock of stories
for when your own dad came back
from the war with nothing to say.

Jilly O'Brien

A LOOK THAT WON'T CATCH ON

Monday 10 May 1621, rue Mouffetard, Paris

Odette clutches my arm on the way back from the markets, shocking me out of my fatigue. Here he comes, the chief physician to Louis XIII, flapping along the high street like an outsized bird in hat and overcoat, boots and gloves, while the crowd parts around him like so many disturbed pigeons. Holding our baskets tight, we press ourselves against the damp stone wall as he passes—the good doctor didn't need his cane to keep us at bay, not with those goggle eyes and beak of a mask—though I can't help noticing what looks like a crack on the left side. I wrinkle my nose at the odour of spices and perfume from the holes in his mask; it was alright for him, all sealed up while the likes of us were exposed daily in the crowded squares and city streets to the miasma, the very air we breathe, whence all disease comes. We exchange a look behind his retreating shiny black leather back— Levantine leather no less, rumour has it … If his patients don't expire from the pestilence, they surely will of fright when he comes to tend them, or more likely scrounge coins out of their desperation. It seems the more unpopular he becomes at court, the wilder his outfits, modelled on the Devil himself. I cross myself quickly, checking the plump fresh aubergines—Madame's favourite—for bruises before hurrying after Odette. Well, there's a look that won't catch on!

Denise O'Hagan

I DO REMEMBER THE WALL

The Monkey Puzzle, a prehistoric tower of a tree, stood at the laneway entrance to my grandmother's farm. As a child I often tried to spot the monkey that must be hiding there and never thought to climb those green-black branches, scratching the sky.

Half a century later, I have questions for my mother.

Why was a Monkey Puzzle, a native of the Andean mountains, in her front garden in Drumagarner? Why was this-must-have garden accessory there alone? Not one like it for miles around. And who chopped it down and what happened to the wood?

I don't know she says *though I do remember the wall ... my father whitewashing the wall.*

He took great pride she says, in the wall that ran alongside the laneway. She remembers him often in early Summer, whitewashing the wall. Standing back to admire the wall, with its black tar footing. Ready for the men marching in Orange. And she's not sure she says, if it was for the men who marched in July, or the ones who marched in August.

He was a good businessman she says

Rosa O'Kane

THE GIRL WHO SAID NO

Her name was Patricia.
She was in my class at junior school and one day she said NO
to the free school milk in the glass bottle that stood all morning in its crate in the
hot summer sun.
NO she said to the teacher.
NO she said to the headmaster.
NO   NO   NO.
Oh   Oh   Oh
She ran from the line-up,
out of the playground,
out of the gate.

It was the day I heard the venetian blinds rattle in the classroom.
Watching each slat cutting the day into long thin slices.
Blinking at patterns of dark and light.
Thinking this moment might go on and on
and on and never end and I was trapped
not like Patricia and her NO.

But I didn't say no.
Not to warm milk,
or to boys with hands that were wet to my touch,
or to the man on a train who sat too close,
or to the man in the car smelling of tweed.

Moya Pacey

NIGHTS WITH ARTHUR

Arthur is my brother we spend a lot of time together we both wear each other's shirts trousers skirts dresses three piece suits denim jackets drain pipe jeans high vis vests skinny jeans crocheted hats leather gloves singlets tailored high waist trousers waistcoats monocles shotguns watches riding boots driving goggles macs coats capes cloaks shorts thongs t shirts rash vests wet suits sweat shirts jumpers anoraks evening dresses upset stomachs headaches wigs toupees glasses short hair long hair pony tail moustaches leg hairs we both have leg hairs. We both have moustaches. We both have such thin arms.

Christine Paice

THERE WERE COCONUTS

(for my mother)

When my whole world ended
I learned to husk a coconut
for there were no more dinners
from fine china on the rosewood
table—but there were coconuts
angled neatly on the ground,
rapped sharp and deft with a mallet,
segment after segment of fibrous
outer skin removed
and the hard roundness struck
(with the blunt edge of a *parang*)
it's all in the precision of that tap—
spilling sour water from two perfect cups—
and then the careful grating of each
half shell on a *parut*
the snowy flesh falling soft and sweet
into the tin plate of my new life …

Anita Patel

THE SPACE WITHIN A TOUCH

silent spring arrives
in winter wind

a virus
microns wide—flees

dying ecosystems, hitches
rides on human breath, thrives

inside the space

        within a touch

masks impede its grasp, steal
the curve of lips, dull

the timbre of a voice
—glass screens receive

fingertips' caress, replace
the warmth of skin

a virus
microns wide—re-contours life, rips

the veil—between
common wealth and self

Yvonne G Patterson

TO FERRY LANDING

i.

thick grey planks worn and cracked
stained with fish guts and oil,
water puckers around the piles
of the old wharf

like the black-backed gull
you came to see the catch
smell the salt and view the crossing

ii.

> *ferry me over*
> *this harbour where I learnt to swim*

water lapping at the boards, boards, boards
and on the other side
the earth waits like an open mouth

the Whitianga estuary flows blue and green
carries the depths that arise in us
we sing your song fearlessly

> *throw a rimu leaf on my casket*
> *with your blessing each spiny twig*
> *helps take me home*

> *as you walk the gravel path back to the river*
> *my folks will see me coming from far away*

Sue Peachey

PATTERNS NOT YET POSSIBLE

The wind slams doors and rattles locks, heralding a gathering of family,
some uncles and children not used to eating at one table.

A boy-child who would say what he saw and saw and saw—
uses the stick to draw more hands in the dirt underfoot.

Chopping carrots, slicing onions and peeling beans
for a stew to feed the little ones still gathering firewood.

An old woman smelling of garlic and cloves sings
a lament of the trees left alone in forests, the canopy lost.

As the wind makes patterns with blossoms, bring
a talking stick to the table and hand it to the old ones first

then the children will hear what it is to describe the hurt
that is carried in bones, from grandma to bairn to patterns in the dirt.

Meredith Pitt

ASHRIDGE FOREST

Sometimes mist would swirl,
soften the darkness
as my father drove me
back to boarding school,
my trunk heavy in the boot,
headlights on high beam.
We hardly spoke, instead
we'd look for fallow deer
eyes shining, ears alert,
seeking out the freshest grass
in moonlit forest clearings.

Once we slowed,
stopped behind a car
to see a doe sprawled
on the tarmac, her eyes
a well of fear, her spindly legs
flailing wildly. Impossible
not to look as the ranger
aimed his rifle, fired,
the shot ringing through
that twilight wood,
cold and hard, the darkness
I had tried so hard to contain
slowly seeping into everything.

Vanessa Proctor

TRUMP AND THE BILLIONAIRES PLAY DIRTY POOL IN THE OVAL OFFICE

with apologies to Gwendolyn Brooks

He not cool. He
damn fool. He

speak hate. He
bad date. He

tweet stink. He
not think. He

well-fed. We
drop dead.

Donna Pucciani

POCKET ROCKS

Dearest, I feel certain that I am going mad again
And I shan't recover this time. I begin to hear voices

tongue songs

And I can't concentrate. So I am doing what seems
the best thing to do. You have given me the greatest possible
happiness, everything has gone from me but the certainty
of your goodness. I cannot go on and spoil your life.

your wife

She smears a jot from the corner of the page on her life

describe

stows the pen; caps the ink looking again
to green nails breaking the crust of soil. She pulls at sleeves, certainly
hooks her brimmed hat; her walking stick. At the door she hears voices:

voice is

muddled inner ear. Tugs on wellingtons, down the path a possible
thing. Touches hardness loosed from dirt, round and smooth against the seam.
More quickly now, her boots on steps, the flowers only seemed
in bloom yesterday, but yesterday was this life

knife

away. A dragonfly cuts glass oscillating paper wings; its possible
song. She reaches for the fluted crag of water, drawing her on again.
And the voices

and the voices and the voices

She notes the spondee, tapping out her stick with certainty.
Again this earth. She shakes loose hardness in grasses and inevitability,
places these pocket rocks against her seeming

flesh, she's weight in utterance

muddle mutter

pulling at bubbles air the vowels of her life

esprit sprite spite

will she float—this time, or sink under—wellingtons & water & the weight of Again.
She has no time but she has the impossible
the thing itself;
fracture as in wood. The air whistles burnt currents, war renewed.
This is the swelling lap of decay. Now, the sun, but now it is
the bassoon of her father, the silted notes of her sister. The brother seems
to reach from the surface as she feels the skin of this death

cessation terminus—

Annunciation:
river rocks add to hard earth, she is here as presented
but there is no one to witness her parting
from this life
once you choose this—anything is possible.
It seems
the water is cold. It is deep again.

KA Rees

RECOVERED

Looking back, I remember, she always said *Where are you from?* Now I understand her need to know the beginning of things. She wanted to take into her own body where my feet had stood in earth, what mud had squished between my toes, the colour of raised dust in sun haloes, acid smell of hot tarmac, cruelty of sharp gravelled country roads on bare feet. This knowledge in her hands, the knowing being the holding, of what was. She wanted to know my *was*, so the map of our present could be correctly aligned.

It wasn't as though my past was there for the taking, I admit. Even if it had been all laid out somewhere, it had long since been covered, palimpsest, papered over, painted out so it looked beige, benign, nothing to see here.

I remember the last day, in the kitchen, cold, gritty lino under our bare feet. And the blankness available for a hesitant new sketching.

I never knew our starting point she said, *so I never knew where we were going, or where we would end up.*

Now, with hindsight, I think she was confusing place with time, skin and body with love, love with land. Land with a starting point.

Sandra Renew

FALLACY OF THE PREDICATE

The 'doer' is merely a fiction added to the deed (Nietzsche)

Nietzsche warns:
There is no 'lightning'

that strikes
There is only the striking

No—*thing* performs this action
Only action itself

[~~She~~ understrike] acts the part
And is stricken from the page

~~She~~ is no longer subject
~~She~~ was never object

~~She~~ is all action
and reiteration

~~She~~ is repetition
~~She~~ is the sum

of all mirrors
repeating

an infinite version
A vision

of herself
for which there is

no original

[~~She~~ strikethrough]
has out-done herself

[~~She~~] is all doing
and undone

[~~She~~] is in-deed
a fiction

written in
after-
       thought

How can she
continue

To remain
Only energy

Light
particle

When will it be time
to strike

[~~She~~] senses
a storm brewing

Sarah Rice

NOLI ME TANGERE

In endless childhood-idle hours I taught myself to
pierce the air with tongue, teeth and fingers
sound owl hoots from cupped hands
blow raspberries from a grass blade
throw a yoyo
tap dance
and
arch each brow at will and eloquently.

Now muffled under dense protective layers,
I draw on the old skills
with a dainty travel step,
or side-mount with my string bag.
And when patience wears,
the black flash of my best Bette Davis,
the warning whiplash
to all who dare
encroach on
my
two
metres.

Marka Rifat

EVE KOSOFSKY SEDGWICK LUNCHING ALONE, 1987

The waiter was polite but firm about extra butter. *Good beginning*, she thinks and scribbles an impatient note on the back of a dirty grocery receipt about the over-importance of smiles. Her ice tea is cold; the waiter is cute. She momentarily questions how she knows these things. Food comes quickly in the middle of her studies. All around her: Good face. Bad face. Face to bruise. Face to kiss. In the far corner two faces across a stained table endlessly fall into each other again and again until they are nothing but laughter and remembrance. She tilts her head and measures love in the way some measure overnight rainfall. Her sandwich is stuffed with suspicion and excess. It tastes of desire. She considers the empty space between a mirror and the reflection before eating. Shifting, she mumbles the declension of hunger as the most banal desire and pushes away her plate. Banal desire grows inside her fire bellows steam-blows through the corridors of her patience. *Bad middle*. She crosses and then uncrosses her legs again. Poor idea. Good idea. Little idea that worms its way into your head and just whispers and whispers. She is still too hot warm bursting, sweat runs down the curve of her back like August. Wiping away the excesses that give way to worry, she raises a finger and asks for the check. As the waiter evaporates into the dimness of too many voices she touches her face and is astounded when her fingers do not burn.

Danielle Rose

20/20

Sixteen years ago, your mother swept past
me in the store, her eyes not dropping

to my belly. That Christmas,
we were not invited, but by the next

—granted entry after birthing their grandson—
I gifted my new parents-in-law

a free standing double picture frame:
my daughter on one side

of the divide, her baby brother on the other.
Next visit, one of my children

buried beneath a cousin. Why didn't
I decry it then, or earlier when, the room

overblown with foreigners now called family,
your father passed his swaddled heir

around and unbound him to admire
the new jewel in his crown. Instead I chose

to push my power with all my power down.
And when the nurse asked if I was *alright, love?*

I should not have acquiesced—
because the stigma, steeped in silence, has festered ever since.

And when I saw your mother in the supermarket today,
it was I who pretended not to see.

Michele Seminara

WOMAN IN THE LINES

most days it is all you are
a layer of starch collared on the inside

a roll-call down hallways
long-laced boots
toeing ends of ties

knuckles fixed tight
to an orderly ledge

what irks us is
left   right   then
left again

we fast on defiance
burn off the old thread

just the same
our right hand raised

to iron out the sting
the cheek of our mouths

as wingless sheets
we fold & are folded again

beneath the camouflage
our sights wiped clean

Ellen Shelley

FOLLY

I really loved the '60s and '70s when life
was so simple and you could slap a woman
on the butt and it was taken as a compliment,

not as sexual harassment[1] I think it is time for us
alpha males to stand up and refuse
to apologise for our gender[2] Women are just

an interest group[3] You have got this bunch
of basically frustrated women who have decided
that if somebody is nude and she is on a poster,

well it's offensive[4] Men should be trained for war,
women for the recreation of the warrior. All else
is folly.[5] What do you think you're looking at,

sugar tits?[6] I will not be harassed by journalists,
even by pretty ones like you. Nick off [7] I don't
have an adverse attitude to women, except

those who are bitches, including my ex-wife …
When she left me she took all the furniture
except the marriage bed. When I woke up in the morning

the first thought I had was, 'Who's going to get my breakfast?'[8]

Melinda Smith

IN THE FUTURE, THEY ATE FROM PLATES OF FINEST PORCELAIN

Of the earth, they are the wretched;
deserving of trough and bog and binding
of sub- and -altern and under-
to break; beneathing and belowing
of less and lessen and less and lessening
of lowering
to gag, to grab, to grope, to goad, to grate.
held in living
and let to dying.
Today, they are in death and of death and deadening and dying.
polluters, they pollute and are polluting and are pollution.
they are it; it-s of a worthless worth unworthily present
in time.
But then
in wait
made human; this dignity in having been
of a people, lost
in antique.
no longer ruining
they were of ruins and rhymes and roads and riddles
and were ruined.
For Tomorrow, they lived and loved and were loving and were lively
they did and they didn't
they were and they were not
they moved and breathed
and they thought
and they needed.

in past—in having passed—a present is given;
that in future, they ate, they did eat, they had eaten
in future, they ate from plates, and
in the future
they ate from plates
of finest porcelain.

Abeir Soukieh

THE WEDDING SUIT

'put on a diaphanous Ossie Clark dress and throw myself off Beachy Head'—Pattie Boyd on her marriage's difficulties

Marriage never held any appeal,
a momentary overwhelming of beauty,
stutter-stepping forward
into the silken fall of unknown.

I chose to remain firm-footed,
a jeans and booted plain Jane
tramping that same landscape,
coupled but truer to myself.

Separation doesn't come any easier
without the gold band,
wanting or deserving nothing.

Alone, the dress feels hard-won,
soft wings to hold me aloft,
and the white cliffs less of a sheer drop.

Gerry Stewart

WAITING

in their eighth decade the sisters remember correct each other sip
sugary mugs of tea on the front verandah balance flowers in their
laps a place rises for us shadowed kitchen and table where their
mother worked where she made everything we wait for the telling
the folding up of the cloth their mother spreading out the tools on
the table to fix the sons' boat we wait it's War in the harbourside
city they wait for the milk delivered twice a day to a tin at the
window for soldiers visiting very welcome for biscuits hospitality it's
open house playing cricket in the lane running from the pro's
children at playtime sorting scraps for metal wearing dog tags to
school name/religion the trench in the playground filled with
rainwater the white-haired mother wearing black walking to the
church next door every day soldiers throwing letters stuffed in
cigarette tins from a ship wanting a pen friend fishing a letter out
writing back writing I am only a child a depth charge Pa said a
depth charge he knew how one sounded running down the stairs
to the bunker waiting there my big sister says she remembers
Grandma's sunny kitchen as a little girl it was a wonderful place
and out the backyard a grassy hill to roll down I waited this long
to visit touch Grandma's rough ring on my wrinkled finger

Sarah St Vincent Welch

THE WALK TO SCHOOL

A response to Occupied Lives, a pictorial essay by
Sophie McNeill, published 6 June 2017

A gravel trudge in early morning;
a walk to school on a day like any other
for five wide-eyed schoolgirls
in these southern Hebron hills.
Do they observe the perfect blue sky,
the hilly stretch of tussock grass,
the curve of the valley?

Or do they watch their own shadows,
or others, longer
that lurk behind occupied windows,
around occupied corners, down occupied alleys?
How many schoolgirls lose their will, their way
skirting threats and malice on their walk to school?

Now, these five stride along,
clutching satchels, escorted by their occupier,
an armed vehicle in front,
two rifled soldiers behind,
who guard against their own.
While five girls walk to school.

Carmel Summers

MY FATHER'S MASK

The stitches in my father's mask grew mild
as Shakespeare, Rembrandt, Brahms wove warp and weft.
He waltzed on satin feet like music's child
and warmed his blood on snow-chilled mountain heft.
To best the bile of poverty and stain
his essence, strong as peppermint, broke out
and spiced the air for others, took the strain
but screened his inner life from prying scout.

Disease decayed his mask, contorted time.
A question mark pervades the voided space.
An answer floats where nature's breezes rhyme
where trunk bark, read as Braille, settles place.
The peace released with whispered final breath
unmasked the light and banished fear of death.

Robyn Sykes

THE SILK ROADS

It's too late to travel them now
so cover me up with Persian rugs
and draw a canopy of silk around my bed.
Slide the bangle of lapis onto my left wrist
and the gold onto the right.
Let no-one forget I drove a Datsun from London to Amritsar
and saw Delphi, the mosque, the pass.
Where the traders have been—I have too.
In with the blood of Europe
there must be that of nomads.
So, bring me a horse.
Let it tattoo the floor with its impatient heels
and dance before me.
As well as your prayers
recite the Diamond Sutra, the Mahabharata
and shout *thus spake Zarathustra*.
Let me breathe my last
with a small statue of Siddhartha in this palm
Sarasvati in that.
Another rug now …
I am unafraid.

Lesley Synge

BRISBANE WATER ESTUARY

At lunch, we talked of matters such as providence and desire—
the fertile plains, the cul-de-sacs. And we celebrated which-
ever benign fate had brought us together so late in our lives.

It was a light-filled day—we shed our cares and floated
on a ferry between mangroves and sandy bays, snatching
at blue skies and heat-dazzle as if we'd never known their like.

From the jetty, we wandered along the water's edge; pelicans
folded on mooring posts, ducks owning the shallows. Shore-side,
a single line of homes—few traces left of the fibro fishing-shacks

and cottages that once defined this battlers' outpost, the end-
point of suburban sprawl. Now, smart re-builds for sea-changers
or investors. We muttered—yet weren't we too, complicit?

As we neared our lunch-stop, someone called out *Look!* and there
we were, the three of us, reflected in a large glass window, laughing
and holding out phones like truant schoolgirls snapping 'selfies'.

Behind us, an intensity of sky and water; sunlight finding
three silver heads—one bright moment, suspended—until
a single kayaker stroked into the frame and life flowed on.

Gillian Telford

READING THE SIGNS IN FNQ

I. VOWS AT PARONELLA PARK

The girls wear sorbet or gelato. Soft frothed fabric, tart
and cool and sweet. Foamed with egg whites.

Their hair, blonded or blacked; their pale shoulders inked
with birds and skulls and butterflies. As if artifice
could exceed themselves, celebrating here
in the mossy turrets of someone else's dream.

They smile in front of Mena Falls; in misted spray, suspended.
And lean on the wall of the pool, where the crocodile stirs, hungry.

II. HENS' WEEKEND PALM COVE

In the swish cafe by the hotel pool
the chicks sit (well-plucked and exfoliated) nearby
the bride-to-be, in mock tiara (rhinestone stilettos).
Her long dark locks; the very straightest of them all.

The chooks (and cheque book) sit apart, all
highlighted roots, and black and white linen.
Italian sandals, of course (sensible heels).

Along the beachside strip, Saturday Harleys promenade;
slow enough to wobble. Cocktail lychees bob in melted ice.
Prawns wilt on plates. Sauces grow skins.

You can read those same signs on the beach, ten steps away
from the chapel. CROCODILES inhabit this area. KEEP AWAY
from the water's edge. DO NOT ENTER the water, no matter
the size of your engagement ring.

Helen Thurloe

SPECIES, MANIFOLD

Inside my hands
a centipede unhooks its feathered feet.

In shiny defiance
her kind are multiplying.

She likes the flavour of sun on bone,
bone on stone, dry, clod-covered stones.

Her eggs. Translucent, licked, pearl light,
they remind me

in this clearing, in the toffee coloured soil
a mother is born every minute.

Under a tree that invites lightning
inside a ground split like mango

she reminds me,
all of the spawning, the arthropods

like trees alight
they mock us

with their thrum, their creamy ovum songs
their bare aching, their bright bare luck.

Catherine Trundle

AN OLIVE ROLLS UNDER THE FRIDGE

For Marika

I've been thinking about intergenerational inheritance of
guilt in the families of perpetrators,
M. weighs in a voice message to me, her Jewish friend.
For example, after the Holocaust

(We are always talking about the Holocaust because of
the anti-racism and genocide education program where
we met, digging through history in Germany and Poland
until we were coated in dirt and spent years writing
letters to each other—she in Germany, I in Canada, then
both of us in England—toiling to clean the dirt out from
our insides.)

but she interrupts
her reflection on the way descendants
of perpetrators may lug guilt
like an albatross
necked about their ancestral pasts, how shame
as other agony can be inherited, to remark
that an olive
has rolled
under the fridge. I imagine
her balancing
the olive jar
the cell phone
the memories now over five years old
and still clawing through
alongside her empathy
unfurling across the line and
this olive
compelling enough
to recess the heart's intimate gatherings
as it rolls recklessly
indifferently
out of
grasp.

Anna Veprinska

COGNATES FOR A FLOODPLAIN

I do not know the word for 'pilgrim' in my grandfather's language,
yet I stand on the riverbank a pilgrim.

On this riverbank, the fishermen call out prices like the ringing of church bells.
Their fish are the size of infants on the verge of speech.
Only—the air, which the fishermen hurl out from their wide-open throats,
has silenced them.

From this riverbank, the boats take flight over the sediment as it laps
against the bank—the same bank that has risen and receded a hundred times
and shifted its weight across half a country.
Each repetition laid down a blanket of silt that, even in the heart of the desert,
never dries.

Beneath this riverbank lie the testimonies of men who marched
nine thousand kilometers over loess and floodwater and starved,
with only blood from their own lips to quench their thirst.
Here, they buried their fear, and the river knows better than to wash away
the footprints they left to mark the grave.

Along this riverbank floated the bodies of poets, their faces as placid
as the clouds, and the boats sent out with sticky rice wrapped in bamboo leaves
to lure the fish away from those bodies—the fish who, amid the sand
and the salt, forgot the difference between flesh
and seed, man and river-grass.

Beside this riverbank float the shells of turtles, not trailed by torn skin
or unlaid eggs but bearing the same water, tinted like the dusk,
in etchings of a language still undefined.

Some villager upstream set these shells in the sand to dry
or hoped they would wash away in the tide, which, even now, reaches farther inland
than I, the pilgrim, will ever go.
Some villager set these shells in the sand and called out the divinations
as clear as the prices of fish.

Maggie Wang

PLASTIQUE IN BRAZIL

The poor have a right
to be beautiful.
The poor suffer so
from asymmetry.

But with a little help, Luisa's face
cuts through the cash economy.
She rises, winged, aerodynamic
her cheeks his masterwork.

I ask: what kind of capital
is beauty? What can it buy?
For those that have no name
and no books to fill their brain
but oh *body!*
your beat and heat, your wile.

When boys dream of soccer scholarships
and girls finger their fat stomachs
and cry. When NGOs go into the favelas
with retired models and cameras and teach
the girls to stick out their
assets, smile.

And if they don't the girls just go down the street
a mile, to the same place Luisa bears his cold hands
at her breast, this god, his cuts a promise
an escape.

The poor have the right to a straight nose.
To big, perfect eyes.
The poor have a right
to rise.

Susan Wardell

ALICE

You are tumbling, down through the rabbit hole, grasping at air, and she is putting you to the test. She asks: *what is the word for that feeling you get when your eyes blur and you see only shadows on your skin?* Dread, you say, and she nods. Then: *The name for white wine that tastes of limestone?* Pass. Which means: fail. You could make up a word, but what would be the point? She is losing interest, checking her phone, glancing across the room. She asks, *What is the word for when you are falling, and the ground is nowhere near; and all you can do is speak out the names of things you know?* You don't answer; all you know is that naming gives us nothing, not even the ground beneath our feet.

Jen Webb

HEY MISTER, YOU HAVE DEVOURED NEARLY ALL OF IT—THIS CAKE

hugely robbed
sharply less
undone   is diminished

its few blueberries
not enough
though hotly purple   its minimal matrix

its last few raisins
beneath the brown crust
not tempting   so   undesirable

listen mister   you didn't ask
left the whole thing wounded
lost   impossible to restore   the sum of it

and   of the rest
too little remains
to nourish my soul   once generous—

I will make more of these
creamed and iced
a delight to the tongue   a festive mix

macadamia
cinnamon   cashew
over red mulled wine   I could offer you

a whole cake   or even two
perhaps another for the road
and we could still be friends   but then

I guess   and sadly fear   you

                        my dream of you

        may not be here tomorrow

              unless ....

Irene Wilkie

HUHU

Fat, white huhu larvae bore   through wood rot:

a skin caster, most edible tātake, who soon grows

wings, legs.   Pepe emerges, flies, circles, lands

on our white weatherboards, then the black fence.

Huhu beetle now, te muimui: sometimes black,

yellow, brown, striped—   eggs again white.

It's nothing to huhu,   this temporary skin—

this   white,   black, yellow, brown,   striped.

Sophia Wilson

STRAPHANGING

Makriyianni, Athens, Greece

The trolleybus has stalled where two familiar streets
agree to meet. Straphanging, I'm jolted to that other
evening in December, rushing to a wedding (mine)
clutching a clichéd red rose, dressed in blue to match
the bruise, empurpled at its epicentre, shadowing my left
eyelid: memento of a dire pre-nuptial falling-out at dead
of night, inflicted accidentally, though nobody will credit that.

It doesn't augur well, but I shall brush aside all auguries
for just an instant as the trolley lurches to a stop.
Straphanging in time, I pause inside an iridescent orb,
detached from every yesterday, all ominous tomorrows.

Suspended for a moment in a trolley at an intersection
while the driver reconnects the cable to its track,
hopefulness is starry-eyed (despite the violet aureole);
those touched by joy can ill afford to look forward or back.

The mustard-yellow Russian trolley lurches like a drunk,
into the zone of doomed relationships and broken trust.
We lived euphorically, though briefly, in our timeless,
glaucous bubble, untroubled by the facts, until illusion cracked.

Now the winds of fortune have reversed chronology
and borne me back, alone, to ride the trolley with the faulty
track. The streets meet at the same blind corner, concealing
from my gaze the days to come, as on that winter
evening of our wedding pact. Today there is the same delay,
without the music and the feast to follow; no bruised eye-
socket, no bridegroom and no lovers' spat. This time
there is only me, a returnee—no rose, no frock—revisiting
the streets our feet once made their own; our lost address.

Raised blinds reveal our filmy drapes the new tenants did not
replace; a person on a mobile phone, twin pots of basil on the sill.

Jena Woodhouse

NOTES

'Foreword, Moya Pacey'. Gloria Steinem's words can be found at: www.elle.com/culture/news/a42331/gloria-steinem-womens-march-speech/

'I will fall sick if you photograph me'. The poem is inspired by a report on the tsunami, 2004, India published by CBS News; 'Man in search of man' is the title of a documentary on the Andaman tribes; 'The age of rising seas' is a quote by writer Rachel Carson.

'On Joy Hester's late portraits of girls'. This poem responds to Joy Hester: *Remember me*, an exhibition which celebrates 100 years since the birth of this significant Australian artist (Heide Museum of Modern Art, Bulleen, Vic.).

'In half light'. *Dressing table (self portrait)*, 1982, painted after the death of Margaret Olley's mother, can be found on the internet.

'Noh'. Noh is a stylised classical Japanese music-drama perfected by Zeami Motokiyo (1363–1443). It recreates ancient legends using elaborate costumes and masks and is believed to suspend actors and audience in a supernatural state.

'The Sea Calls My Name' is an ekphrastic work written in response to a literary project between The Hunter Writers Centre and The Newcastle Art Gallery where writers read their work in response to James Drinkwater's exhibition of paintings *the sea calls me by name*.

'X300'. Bangarra Dance Theatre's response to nuclear testing on Maralinga Tjarutja traditional lands in Central Australia in the 1950s.

'Playing Dead'. Female dragonflies feign death to avoid stalking males.

'Just Before Covid-19 Hits I Sell My Gold'. Sam Wagan Watson, 'tigerland', *Smoke Encrypted Whispers* (UQP, 2004).

'The crystal masks of Lynette and Donald'. Australian virtual reality filmmaker Lynette Wallworth received a Crystal Award at the World Economic Forum in Davos, January 2020. Crystal awards celebrate the achievements of artists whose leadership inspires inclusive and sustainable change.

'Bodhi of a poem'. 'Bodhi' means awakening or enlightenment.

'A look that won't catch on'. Charles de Lorme (1584–1678), French physician to Louis XIII, is credited with inventing (c. 1619) the first 'plague doctor' costume worn by physicians during the second wave of the bubonic plague in Europe.

'Pocket Rocks'. The first stanza of this sestina (except italicised lines) is paraphrased from the text of Virginia Woolf's suicide note, which was influenced in part by an extract published by the Associated Press, 19 April 1941: 'Mrs. Woolf's Body Found: Verdict of Suicide Is Returned in Drowning of Novelist'.

'Fallcy of the predicate'. Epigraph: Judith Butler quotes from Nietzsche's *On the Genealogy of Morals*, and adds 'There is no gender identity behind the expressions of gender' (Judith Butler, *Gender Trouble*, Routledge, 1990).

'Folly'. This poem is composed of public statements nominated for Ernie Awards for Sexist Behaviour (www.ernies.com.au/) in their respective years. Full details in *The Ernies Book: 1000 Terrible Things Australian Men Have Said About Women* (Meredith Burgmann and Yvette Andrews, Allen & Unwin, 2007). The specific sources of the quotes in the poem are as follows: (1) Kirk Pengilly (former INXS band member), 2018, www.smh.com.au/entertainment/former-inxs-star-kirk-pengilly-says-he-misses-slapping-a-woman-on-the-butt-20171130-gzwd06.html; (2) Sen. David Leyonhjelm, during an appearance on Sky News' *Outsiders* program, interviewed by Rowan Dean and Ross Cameron, 1 July 2018; (3) Mark Latham, federal Labor MP, 2002; (4) Mark Patrick, advertising agent, 1997; (5) John Justice, president of the Campbelltown branch of the Young Liberals, 1997; (6) Mel Gibson, actor, 2006; (7) Paul Keating, former Prime Minister, 2007; (8) John Phillips, pensioner, 2002, who unsuccessfully sued the NSW Attorney-General for harm inflicted on him by up to 100 women in government departments.

'In the Future, they Ate from Plates of Finest Porcelain'. *This title comes from the Larissa Sansour film (2015) and photo exhibition (2017) of the same name.*

'Plastique in Brazil'. This poem is an interpretation of the ethnographic context of plastic surgery in Brazil, as presented in the journal article A. Edmonds (2007), '"The Poor Have the Right to Be Beautiful": Cosmetic surgery in neoliberal Brazil', *Journal of the Royal Anthropological Institute*, 13(2): 363–81. The line 'the poor have a right to be beautiful' was drawn from the article's title; all other wording and narrative details are the author's own.

ACKNOWLEDGEMENTS

'Rhythmic Oscillations' was published in *Not Very Quiet* (2019) and in *Density of Compact Bone* (Ginninderra Press, 2021).

'Waiting for Imran Khan' was runner-up in the 2015 University of Canberra Vice-Chancellor's International Poetry Prize and published in the prize anthology that year. It was also published in *Earth Girls* (Pitt Street Poetry 2016) and in *Not Very Quiet* (2019).

'In one hundred days' was published in *Not Very Quiet* (2018) and in *out of emptied cups* (Salmon Poetry, 2019).

'Tricks of the Trade' was published in *Not Very Quiet* (2020) and included in *the moment, taken* (Recent Work Press, 2021).

'The dusky grasswren' was published in *Not Very Quiet* (2019) and in *Utterly* (Ginninderra Press, 2020).

'Interior with wardrobe mirror' was published in *Not Very Quiet* (2018) and in *Intermittent Angels* (Girls on Key, 2020).

'Scar massage' was published in *Not Very Quiet* (2018), *Australian Poetry Anthology* (eds Yvette Holt and Magan Magan, 2019), and in *Autobiochemistry* (UWA Publishing, 2019).

'Black Dream Bird' was published in *Not Very Quiet* (2018) and in *Bone House* (Doire Press, 2021).

'Woman Quits Femininity' was published in *Not Very Quiet* (2019) and in *Far and Wild* (Flying Island Books, 2021).

'All the willing hours' was published in *Not Very Quiet* (2017); in *Exhilaration*, Newcastle Poetry at the Pub 2017; in *Brew*, 30 years of Poetry at the Pub Newcastle 1988—2017; in *On First Looking* (Puncher & Wattmann, 2018); and in *Green Point Bearings* (Ginninderra Press, 2018).

'Letter to a bride to be' was published in *Not Very Quiet* (2019) and in *Speculate: A collection of microlit* (with Eugen Bacon, Meerkat Press, 2021).

'The Sea Calls My Name' was published in *Not Very Quiet* (2019) and in *Newcastle Poetry at the Pub* (eds Geoffrey Nicholls and Jill McKeowe, 2020).

'Where We Go' was published in *Not Very Quiet* (2019) and in *A History of What I'll Become* (UWAP, 2020).

'from the garlic wife' was published in *Not Very Quiet* (2020) and in *Inheritance* (Puncher & Wattmann, 2021).

'Disarming' was published in *Not Very Quiet* (2019) and in *F-Words* (Recent Work Press, 2021).

'In the Dutch tradition' was published in *Not Very Quiet* (2018) and in *The Long Beds* (Carcanet Press, 2020).

'Diapause' was published in *Not Very Quiet* (2020) and in *The Wear of My Face* (Spinifex Press, 2021).

'Camille Claudel' was published in *Not Very Quiet* (2019) and in *No News* (Recent Work Press, 2020).

'August in Lahore' was published in *Not Very Quiet* (2019) and in *The Djinn Hunters* (Rabbit Poets Series, 2021).

'The girl who said NO' was published in *Not Very Quiet* (2019) and in *Doggerland* (Recent Work Press, 2020).

'20/20' was published in *Not Very Quiet* (2020) and *Suburban Fantasy* (UWA Publishing, 2021).

'Folly' was published in *Not Very Quiet* (2019) and *Listen, bitch* (Recent Work Press, 2019) and *Man-handled* (Recent Work Press, 2020).

'The Silk Roads' was published in *Not Very Quiet* (2020) and was included in the Queensland Poetry Festival's Panacea Poets series (2020).

'Brisbane Water Estuary' was published in *Not Very Quiet* (2018) and *Midnight Lexicon*, a Picaro Poets chapbook (Ginninderra Press, 2020).

'Alice' was published in *Not Very Quiet* (2018) and in *The Six Senses* by the Authorised Theft collective (Cassandra Atherton, Paul Hetherington, Paul Munden, Jen Webb, Jordan Williams) (Recent Work Press, 2019).

'Straphanging' was published in *Not Very Quiet* (2020) and in *AAIA* [Australian Archaeological Institute at Athens] Newsletter No. 16, November 2020.

CONTRIBUTORS

Cassandra Atherton is an international expert on prose poetry. Cassandra co-wrote *Prose Poetry: An Introduction* and co-edited *The Anthology of Australian Prose Poetry* with Paul Hetherington. She is a commissioning editor for *Westerly* magazine and associate editor at MadHat Press (USA).

Oakley Ayden (she/her) is an autistic, bisexual American writer from North Carolina. Her poems appear in *Ghost City Review, Maw: Poetry Journal, The Cabinet of Heed, Brave Voices Magazine, Sledgehammer Literary Journal, Neologism Poetry Journal* and elsewhere. She lives in California's San Bernardino National Forest with her two daughters.

Magdalena Ball is a novelist, poet, reviewer and interviewer, and is the managing editor of Compulsive Reader. She has been widely published in literary journals and anthologies and is the author of a number of books of poetry and fiction, the latest of which is *Density of Compact Bone* (Ginninderra Press, 2021).

J V Birch lives in Adelaide. Her poems have been anthologised, exhibited, performed and published in Australia, the UK, Canada and the US. She has three chapbooks with Ginninderra Press and a full-length collection, *more than here*. Visit www.jvbirch.com to read more of her work.

Wendy BooydeGraaff is the author of *Salad Pie*, a children's picture book (Ripple Grove Press, 2016). Her work has been included in *Meniscus* (2020), *Lily Poetry Review* (2021), *CutBank Online* (2021), *NOON* (2021), and elsewhere. Originally from Ontario, Canada, she now lives in Michigan, United States.

Emily Bourke is a Canberra-based poet from Brisbane, who enjoys writing about ecology and love of place. She uses the natural world to ground the emotions of her poems.

Devika Brendon is a writer, teacher, editor, columnist and reviewer. Her poetry, short stories and literary reviews are extensively published internationally. Her opinion pieces are published in *Ceylon Today* and *The Sunday Island*. Devika is an editor with *Girls On Key*, and Consultant Content Editor for the SEALA Global Network

Michelle Brock lives near the Molonglo Gorge on the outskirts of Queanbeyan and enjoys writing short stories and poetry, including various forms of tanka. She is a member of the Lyrebird Tanka Circle and her tanka, tanka prose and haiga appear regularly in Australian and overseas journals and anthologies.

Lisa Brockwell was born and raised in Sydney and spent a large chunk of her early adult life in London. She now lives in Scotland. Her poems have been published in the *Spectator*, the *Canberra Times*, the *Weekend Australian*, *Meanjin* and *The Best Australian Poems*. Her first book, *Earth Girls* (Pitt Street Poetry) was commended in the Anne Elder Award. *The Round Ring* (Pitt Street Poetry) is forthcoming in 2021.

Denise Burton has been writing poetry for 40 years, most of which is published in her recent anthology, *If I Were a Poet*; the remainder is hiding in the bottom drawer. She enjoys the simplicity of words and ideas that can be achieved in poetry. Originally from Sydney, she now regards Canberra as home.

Monica Carroll writes and makes things.

Anne Casey is a journalist, magazine editor, legal author and media communications director. She is an internationally award-winning Irish poet/writer living in Australia. Author of four critically acclaimed collections, her work is widely published, ranking in the *Irish Times*' Most Read. She can be found at anne-casey.com or @1annecasey.

Jhilam Chattaraj is an academic and poet based in Hyderabad, India. Her works have been published at *Room*, *Porridge*, *Burrow*, *Queen Mob's Tea House*, *Colorado Review*, *World Literature Today* and *Asian Cha* among others. *Noise Cancellation* (Hawakal Publishers, 2021) is her latest book of poems.

Eileen Chong is a Sydney poet and the author of nine books. Her work has been shortlisted for the NSW Premier's, the Victorian Premier's, and twice for the Prime Minister's Literary Awards. Her most recent book is *A Thousand Crimson Blooms* from UQP. She lives and works on unceded Gadigal land of the Eora Nation.

Emilie Collyer lives on Wurundjeri land, where she writes poetry, plays and prose. Her writing has been widely published. Award-winning plays include *Contest*, *Dream Home* and *The Good Girl*, which has had multiple international productions. She is currently undertaking a PhD at RMIT, where she is researching feminist creative practice.

Jennifer Compton lives in Melbourne. Her work has appeared in *The Best Australian Poetry* (2003 and 2009) and in *The Best Australian Poems* (2004, 2005, 2008, 2011, 2012, 2013, 2014, 2015 and 2017). And in *The Best of Best New Zealand Poems* (2011). Her collection *the moment, taken* was published in 2021 (Recent Work Press, Canberra).

PS Cottier is a Canberra poet, who also reviews books, and sometimes writes essays and fiction. She is poetry editor at the *Canberra Times*, and wrote a PhD at the Australian National University on images of animals in the works of Charles Dickens.

MTC Cronin has published over twenty books (poetry, prose poems and essays), a number of which have appeared in translation.

Jan Dean lives on Awabakal country. Her writing is represented in *Meanjin, Southerly, Rabbit: a journal of non-fiction poetry* and *Verity La*. She won the 2019 Senior Poetry at the Lane Cove Literary Awards, and the 2018 joanne burns competition, Hunter category. Her latest collection is *Intermittent Angels* (Girls on Key, 2020).

Tricia Dearborn is a Sydney poet, writer and editor. Her latest books are *Autobiochemistry* (UWA Publishing, 2019) and *She reconsiders life on the run* (IPSI Chapbooks, 2019). Her work is widely represented in anthologies, including *The Anthology of Australian Prose Poetry* and *Contemporary Australian Poetry*. She was a judge of the 2019 University of Canberra Vice-Chancellor's International Poetry Prize. She was the winner of the 2021 Neilma Sidney Short Story Prize.

Sally Denshire is an Anglo-Australian writer living on Wiradjuri land. She has recent poems in *fourW* (2016, 2017, 2018, 2019), *Riparian, Not Very Quiet* and *Poetry for the Planet: An Anthology of Imagined Futures* and reviews in *realtime* and *Plumwood Mountain*. Her PhD from the University of Technology, Sydney was autoethnographic.

Moyra Donaldson is a poet and creative writing facilitator from Co. Down, Northern Ireland. She has published nine collections of poetry; her most recent is *Bone House* (Doire Press, 2021). In 2019, she received a Major Individual Artist award from the Arts Council of Northern Ireland.

Jane Downing's poetry has appeared in *Cordite, Rabbit,* the *Canberra Times, Eureka Street, Bluepepper, Not Very Quiet, The Best Australian Poems* (2004 and 2015), and elsewhere. Her collection, *When Figs Fly* was published by Close-Up Books in 2019.

Natasha Dust is a student at the University of Sydney, where she studies arts and sciences. She lives with her family and an assortment of other grumpy animals, and has been writing poetry since she was nine years old. She hopes to publish a collection sometime in the future.

Eugenie Edquist is a poet who lives and works in Canberra, Australia. She has been published in *Not Very Quiet*, has featured for *Girls on Key*, and has shared her work at events throughout ACT and the region. She's happy to be part of Canberra's thriving and generous poetry community.

Anne Elvey is a poet, editor and researcher, living on Boonwurrung Country in bayside Melbourne (Naarm). Her poetry publications include *Obligations of voice* (2021), *On arrivals of breath* (2019), *White on White* (2018) and *Kin* (2014). Her most recently scholarly work is *Reading the Magnificat in Australia: Unsettling Engagements* (2020).

Diane Fahey is the author of thirteen poetry collections, *November Journal* the most recent. She has won major poetry awards and has received literary grants from the Australia Council. Her poetry has been represented in over seventy anthologies. Diane holds a PhD in Creative Writing from UWS. dianefaheypoet.com

Amelia Fielden is a professional translator of Japanese literature. Nine collections of her own poetry have been published. She has collaborated with other poets to produce six further collections, and edited or co-edited ten anthologies. Twenty-five books of her translations are in print, including the award-winning *Ferris Wheel*, an anthology of modern Japanese tanka.

Ellie Fisher is a poet and undergrad English and History student at the University of Western Australia (Kinjarling/Albany). She has been published by or has work forthcoming with *Not Very Quiet*, *Westerly*, *Aniko Magazine*, *Pelican Magazine*, Night Parrot Press, *Damsel*, and *Peafowl Magazine*.

Anna Forsyth is a poet and editor originally from New Zealand, now living in New South Wales. She is the founder of feminist poetry organisation Girls on Key Poetry, where she is the editor of the small press. Her work has appeared in print and online, including in *FourW*, *Not Very Quiet*, *Poetry NZ*, *Headland* and *Landfall*. Her latest poetry collection is entitled *Beatific Toast*.

Jane Frank's latest chapbook is *Wide River* (Calanthe Press, 2020). Her work is widely published and anthologised, most recently in *Westerly*, *StylusLit*, *Shearsman*, *Burrow*, *Live Encounters*, *Poetry for the Planet* (Litoria Press, 2021), *Grieve* vol 9 (Hunter Writers Centre, 2021) and *Meridian* (APWT/Drunken Boat, 2020). She lives in Brisbane and teaches creative and professional writing at Griffith University.

Irina Frolova is a Russian-Australian poet who lives on the Awabakal land with her three children and two fur babies. Her first collection of poetry *Far and Wild* was released by Flying Island Books in January 2021. You can find Irina on Facebook at @irinafrolovapoet or on Instagram @far_and_wild_poetry.

Kathryn Fry has poems in *Antipodes* (2016, 2019), *Cordite Poetry Review* (2016), *Not Very Quiet* (2017–2020 incl.), *Westerly* (2019, 2020) and *Science Write Now* (2020). Her collections are *Green Point Bearings* (Ginninderra Press, 2018) and *The Earth Will Outshine Us* (Ginninderra Press, 2021).

Sophie Furlong Tighe is a poet from Dublin. You can find their work in *ROPES, Sonder, Wax Nine,* and *Variant Lit,* among other places. They were the editor of *Icarus* magazine's 71st volume. They tweet @furtiso

Allison Goldstein received her MFA from California College of the Arts. She has been published in a variety of literary and cultural publications including *Burnt Pine, Gyroscope Review,* and *Maximum Rock'n'Roll.* Allison currently lives and writes in South Florida with her husband and two cats.

Hazel Hall's recent collections are *Step by Step,* with tai chi master Angie Egan (Picaro Poets, 2019), *Moonrise Over the Siding* with Parkinson's Artists (Interactive Press, 2019), and *Severed Web,* with artist Deborah Faeyrglenn (Picaro Poets, 2020) and a verse drama on health care, *Please Add Your Signature and Date it Here* (Litoria Press, 2021).

Kristin Hannaford is an Australian poet and short fiction writer. She lives in Yeppoon, Central Queensland and has published four collections of poetry; the most recent is *Curio* (Walleah Press, 2014). Kristin's work features in the Queensland Poetry Festival's 2020 'Panacea Poets' program and featured as a sound installation for the 2021 Village Festival.

Michelle Hartman is the author of four books available on Amazon, along with three chapbooks. Hartman's work can be found online, in multiple journals in America and various countries overseas. She is the former editor of *Red River Review,* and co-owner of The Hungry Buzzard Press.

Belgian-born author **Dominique Hecq** lives in Melbourne. Hecq writes across genres and sometimes across tongues. Her works include a novel, four collections of short stories and eleven books of poetry. *Tracks* (2020) and *Songlines* (2021) are her latest poetry offerings. With Eugen Bacon, she co-authored *Speculate* (2021), a collection of microlit. A runner-up in the 2021 Carmel Bird Digital Award, *Smacked* is fresh off the press.

Gail Hennessy is a poet, writer and researcher who has been published widely in national and regional newspapers, literary and academic journals and anthologies. She has produced three books of poetry: *Witnessing* (self published, 2009), *Written on Water* (Flying Island Books, 2017) and *The M Word* (Girls on Key, 2019).

Jill Jones' most recent books include *Wild Curious Air,* winner of the 2021 Wesley Michel Wright Prize, *A History of What I'll Become,* which was shortlisted for the 2021 Kenneth Slessor Award, and *Viva the Real,* which was shortlisted for the 2019 Prime Minister's Literary Award for Poetry and the 2020 John Bray Award.

Michaela Keeble is a white Australian writer living in Aotearoa with her partner and kids. Her poetry has been published and anthologised widely, including in *Intimate Relations: Communicating in the Anthropocene* (Lexington Press, 2021) and a forthcoming climate collection with Auckland University Press. She has a children's book, co-authored with her son, coming out with Gecko Press in early 2022.

Kathy Kituai, the founder and facilitator of Limestone Tanka Poets, 2010–2021, has published an NBC documentary, seven poetry collections, a CD, five anthologies, a children's story, and received two Canberra Critic awards for her teaching in Scotland and Australia since 1990. *Deep in the Valley of Tea Bowls* won an ACT Publishing and Writing Award.

Kimberly Lambright is the author of *ULTRA-CABIN*, winner of the 42 Miles Press Poetry Award. Her work appears in *OAR*, *Phoebe*, *Columbia Poetry Review*, *Sink Review*, *ZYZZYVA*, *Bear Review*, *Bone Bouquet*, *The Boiler*, *Little Patuxent Review*, the *Burnside Review*, and elsewhere. She lives in Brooklyn, New York.

Robyn Lance's poetry has been aired on ABC Radio National and displayed on Canberra's buses and telegraph poles, on steel plates in regional NSW, on paper, online and on exhibition walls.

Penelope Layland is an award-winning Canberra poet whose work has appeared in Australian and international journals. Her most recent book is *Nigh* (Recent Work Press, 2020).

Nellie Le Beau is the winner of the 2020 Puncher & Wattmann Prize for a First Book of Poetry. Her collection *Inheritance* (Puncher & Wattmann) will be published in late 2021. She is a Wheeler Centre Hot Desk Fellow and a PhD candidate in poetry.

Wes Lee lives in New Zealand. Her poetry has appeared in *Best New Zealand Poems*, *Westerly*, *Cordite* and *Australian Poetry Journal*, among others. Her latest poetry collection, *By the Lapels*, was launched in 2019 (Steele Roberts Aotearoa). Most recently she was awarded the Poetry New Zealand Prize 2019 by Massey University Press.

Rosanna E Licari won the 2021 AAALS Poetry Prize. Her work has appeared in *The Anthology of Australian Prose Poetry* (MUP, 2020), *Scars: an anthology of microlit* (Spineless Wonders, 2020) and *Pulped Fiction: an anthology of microlit* (Spineless Wonders, 2021). She teaches English to refugees and migrants, and is the poetry editor of *StylusLit*.

Miriam Wei Wei Lo writes to probe the gap between what is and what should be. Find her on Insta @miriamweiweilo or in Western Australia on Whadjuk Noongar Boodja, where she teaches creative writing at Sheridan Institute.

LindaAnn LoSchiavo is a writer, dramatist, and poet. She is an Elgin Award winner and her latest poetry titles are *A Route Obscure and Lonely* and *Concupiscent Consumption*. Recently named Poetry SuperHighway's Poet of the Week, she is a member of the Science Fiction and Fantasy Poetry Association and the Dramatists Guild. She tweets @Mae_Westside

Kate Lumley's poetry has been published in journals *Studio, Not Very Quiet, Rochford Street Review* and in anthologies including *Australian Love Poems 2013, Prayers of a Secular World* (2016); *To end all wars* (Puncher & Wattmann, 2018), *Avant la letter* (2020), *From the Embers* (2020), *Australian Poetry Collection* (2020) and *9,000 miles away* (2021).

Julie Maclean is the author of four pamphlets and one full collection. She lives on the Surf Coast in Victoria. www.juliemacleanwriter.com

Jacqui Malins is a poet and artist based in Canberra. She has featured at the Woodford Festival and National Folk Festival, and was an Australian Poetry Slam finalist in 2015. She has published a chapbook, *Cavorting with Time* (Recent Work Press, 2018), and her first collection is *F-Words* (Recent Work Press, 2021).

Sameeya Maqbool is a British-Pakistani Muslim literary scholar and poet, born and raised in Lancashire. She is a second-year PhD candidate in English Literature at Lancaster University. Her poems have appeared in *SPAM zine & Press, Ta Voix*, and *The Selkie*.

Jennifer Kemarre Martiniello is an award winning poet of Arrernte, Chinese and Anglo-Celtic descent. She founded the ACT Indigenous Writers Group in 1999. She is published in national and international journals and anthologies including *Macquarie PEN Anthology of Australian Literature*.

Victoria McGrath is a poet from Yass, New South Wales who has been widely published in journals and anthologies in Australia and the US, including *The Best Australian Poems* (twice). She has been awarded in a number of competitions, nominated for the US Best of the Net award, and was shortlisted for the Newcastle Poetry Prize.

Kate Miller is English and, until lockdown, a Londoner. *The Observances* (Carcanet, 2015) won the Seamus Heaney Centre Prize for a First Collection. No stranger to cross-arts collaboration, she works with other artists on audio-visual and live events based on poems from *The Long Beds* (Carcanet, 2020) and new commissions. She is online at katemiller.me

Rosalind Moran is a writer of fiction, non-fiction, and poetry. Her work has been published in *Reader's Digest*, *Meanjin*, *Overland*, *Kill Your Darlings*, and *The Global Youth Review*, among others. In 2019, she was a runner-up for the June Shenfield Poetry Award. and a finalist in the 2021 Cambridge Poetry and Prose Prize. She is also a co-founder of *Cicerone Journal*.

Lizz Murphy writes between Binalong, NSW and Canberra, ACT. She has published 14 books of different kinds including nine poetry titles. Her latest poetry collection is *The Wear of My Face* (Spinifex Press, 2021). Her other Spinifex titles are *Two Lips Went Shopping* and the popular anthology *Wee Girls: Women Writing from an Irish Perspective*. She is widely published internationally and blogs at lizzmurphypoet.blogspot.com

K A Nelson is a Canberra poet who was one of several guest editors for *Not Very Quiet*. Recent Work Press published her first collection, *Inlandia*, in 2018. She has won, or been shortlisted for prizes such as the Judith Wright Poetry Prize for New and Emerging Poets (2010), the Gwen Harwood Poetry Prize (2012) and the NT Writers Centre Poetry Award (2014). Her work appears in several anthologies including *Best Australian Poems* (2015).

Gemma Nethercote Way lives in Canberra. Her poetry has previously been published in *Not Very Quiet*, *Meniscus*, and *Axon*. She was a contributor to the 2020 anthology *No News* (Recent Work Press), and was shortlisted for the 2019 Anne Edgeworth Emerging Writer's Fellowship.

Nadia Niaz is a writer and academic whose work investigates multilingual creative expression, particularly in poetry, the practicalities and politics of translation, and language use among globally mobile cohorts. She's the founder and editor of the *Australian Multilingual Writing Project* and the author of *The Djinn Hunters*.

Jenni Nixon's poetry collections are: *swimming underground* (Ginninderra Press, 2015) and *café boogie* (Interactive Press, 2004). She has been anthologised in *Southerly*, *Cordite*, *Rochford Street Review*, *I Protest*, *Milestones*, *Musings During a Time of Pandemic*, *I Can't Breathe*, and *Kistrech* (Kenya). A new collection is on the way.

Jilly O'Brien is an award-winning poet from Aotearoa New Zealand. She has had poems published in journals such as *Landfall*, *Stand*, *Mayhem*, *Cordite*, *Takahē*,

Catalyst, and has had her poetry displayed on the ice in Antarctica, in libraries in Quebec, on benches and bookmarks in Dunedin and on the back of parking tickets.

Denise O'Hagan is an award-winning editor and poet. Based in Sydney, she has a background in commercial book publishing. Her poetry is published widely and has received numerous awards, most recently the Dalkey Poetry Prize 2020. Her debut poetry collection, *The Beating Heart*, is published by Ginninderra Press (2020). denise-ohagan.com

Rosa O'Kane is an emerging poet who was born and grew up in Northern Ireland. Her poem 'Hydrography of the Heart' was a commended entry in the Hippocrates Prize 2014. She has been shortlisted for the ACU Poetry Prize in 2018 and 2019. Her poems have been published in *Axon Journal*, *Not Very Quiet*, *Blue Nib* and the *Canberra Times*. Rosa lives and works in Canberra.

Moya Pacey published her third collection, *Doggerland*, with Recent Work Press in 2020. Her previous collections *Black Tulips* and *The Wardrobe* were shortlisted for the ACT Writers Centre Poetry Award. She lives in Canberra, Australia.

Christine Paice is an award-winning poet and writer. She has published two poetry collections, *Mad Oaks* and *Staring at the Aral Sea*, a children's book, *The Great Rock Whale* (Hachette Australia, 2009) and her debut novel, *The Word Ghost* (Allen & Unwin, 2014). Her work has been shortlisted, anthologised, and performed on BBC Radio.

Anita Patel is a Canberra writer. Her poetry collection, *A Common Garment*, was published in 2019 (Recent Work Press). Her work also appears in publications such as *Cordite Poetry Review*, *Mascara Literary Review* and *Australian Poetry Anthology* (Vol. 8, 2020). She was the guest editor for Issue 2 of *Not Very Quiet*.

Yvonne G Patterson lives in Perth, Western Australia, is from New Zealand and enjoys poetry after a career in human services policy and clinical psychology. She was commended in the 2018 National Tom Collins Poetry Prize, has poems published in anthologies and journals and is in the WA Poets Emerging Writers 2021–23 program.

Sue Peachey is a New Zealander living in Canberra. She has been published in *Cordite*, *Westerly*, *Not Very Quiet*, *Eucalypt*, *Haibun Today* and *Kokako*.

Meredith Pitt is a Blue Mountains based poet. She has honed her craft through attendance of numerous workshops and the occasional residential course. Her work has been published in various online and print journals and anthologies. Meredith was awarded the Verandah 2018 Literary Award.

Vanessa Proctor is immediate past president of the Australian Haiku Society. Her poetry has appeared in journals such as *Australian Poetry Journal, Island, Meanjin, Meniscus* and *Southerly*, and has also been carved in stone, printed on teabag labels and set to music.

Donna Pucciani, a Chicago-based writer, has published poetry worldwide in *Shi Chao Poetry, Poetry Salzburg, ParisLitUp, Mediterranean Poetry, Acumen, Meniscus, Gradiva*, and other journals. She has received awards from the Illinois Arts Council, the National Federation of State Poetry Societies, and others. Her seventh book of poems is *EDGES* (Purple Flag, 2016).

KA Rees is a writer of short fiction and poetry. Her work has been widely published, including by *Australian Poetry, Cordite Poetry Review, Kill Your Darlings*, Margaret River Press, *Overland, Review of Australian Fiction*, Spineless Wonders and *Yalobusha Review*. Her debut poetry collection is *Come the Bones* published by Flying Island Press (2021).

Sandra Renew's recent collections are *It's the sugar, Sugar* (Recent Work Press, 2021) and *Acting Like a Girl* (Recent Work Press, 2019; winner of the 2020 ACT Writing and Publishing Award for Poetry, and shortlisted for the ACT Book of the Year 2020). Sandra and Moya Pacey (founding co-editors of *Not Very Quiet* online journal) were awarded a Canberra Critics Circle Award in 2019 for their influential contribution to women's poetry.

Sarah Rice's poetry collection, *Fingertip of the Tongue*, won the Eyelands International Book Awards and was shortlisted in the ACT Publishing Awards. Sarah won the Ron Pretty and Bruce Dawe, and co-won the Writing Ventures, and Gwen Harwood poetry prizes. She has been shortlisted in numerous national and international writing awards.

Marka Rifat lives in Scotland and is the commended author in The Toulmin Prize 2020 and runner-up in the 2021 Janet Coats Memorial Prize. She is a member of Mearns Writers. Her poetry, fiction and essays have been included in anthologies published in the UK, USA and now Australia.

Danielle Rose is the author of *at first & then* and *The History of Mountains*. Her work can be found at Palette, Hobart, and Pithead Chapel.

Michele Seminara is a poet from Sydney and managing editor of online creative arts journal *Verity La*. Her books include *Engraft* (Island Press, 2016), *Scar to Scar* (with Robbie Coburn, PressPress, 2016), *HUSH* (Blank Rune Press, 2017), and *Suburban Fantasy* (UWA Publishing, 2021). Find more at micheleseminara.net

Ellen Shelley is from Newcastle, NSW. She has been published in *Eureka, Backstory, Other Terrain, Not Very Quiet, Eucalypt,* the *Canberra Times, Cordite, Dámour, Australian Poetry Collaboration, UNFURL* online and the *Blue Nib*. She was Highly Commended for the Philip Bacon Ekphrasis Poetry Award (2019) and participated in It's Raining Poetry in Adelaide.

Melinda Smith is a poet, editor and teacher who lives and writes in the ACT, on Ngunnawal Country. Her latest book is *Man-handled* (Recent Work Press, 2020), and she is the author of seven other poetry books, including the 2014 Prime Minister's Literary Award winner, *Drag down to unlock or place an emergency call.*

Abeir Soukieh is a Lebanese-Australian poet and writer who was born and raised in Canberra. Her work can be found in *Cordite Poetry Review, Not Very Quiet, Australian Poetry Anthology* (2020) and elsewhere. She is currently completing a Graduate Diploma in Psychological Science through Deakin University.

Sarah St Vincent Welch is a Canberra-based writer. Her poetry chapbook *OPEN* was published in 2019 (Rochford Press). *chalk borders* is forthcoming in early 2022 as part of Flying Islands Pocket Books of Poetry series (Cerberus Press). She is the founder of kindredtrees.com.au Canberra trees and poetry project.

Gerry Stewart is a poet, creative writing tutor and editor based in Finland. Her poetry collection, *Post-Holiday Blues,* was published by Flambard Press, UK. *Totems* is forthcoming from Hedgehog Poetry Press in 2021. Her writing blog is at thistlewren.blogspot.fi/ and she is @grimalkingerry on Twitter.

Carmel Summers' first book of responsive tanka, *The last day before snow,* written with eight Australian poets, won the ACT Publisher's Award for Poetry in 2017. Her work appears in a number of collections and journals, in Australia and overseas. She is a PhD student at the University of Canberra.

Robyn Sykes is published in journals and anthologies nationally, internationally and online, including three times in *Not Very Quiet*. Nature, human behaviour and a BSc (Hons) inform her work, which she enjoys presenting on stage. Robyn coordinates A Brush with Poetry in Binalong, near Canberra.

Lesley Synge holds an MA in Creative Writing from the University of Queensland. Her poetry collections are *Mountains Belong to the People Who Love Them, Organic Sister* and *Signora Bella's Grand Tour*. She also publishes fiction and non-fiction, for which she has won a number of awards.

Gillian Telford, a NSW poet, has three published collections: *Moments of Perfect Poise* (Ginninderra Press, 2008), *An Indrawn Breath* (Picaro Press, 2015) and *Midnight Lexicon*, a Picaro Poets chapbook (Ginninderra Press, 2020). Her work is widely published in journals and anthologies including *Not Very Quiet* (2018, 2019) and Grieve Anthologies (Hunter Writers Centre 2016–18, 2020).

Helen Thurloe is a Sydney poet and author. Her poems have received many awards, including the ACU Literature Prize and the Quantum Words Science Poetry Competition. Helen's debut novel, *Promising Azra*, was shortlisted for the 2017 NSW Premier's Literary Awards.

Catherine Trundle is a writer and anthropologist based in Wellington, New Zealand. She has had poetry published in *Landfall, Takahē, Poetry New Zealand Yearbook, Blackmail Press*, and *Plumwood Mountain*.

Anna Veprinska is a Canadian poet and scholar. She has published the books *Empathy in Contemporary Poetry after Crisis* (Palgrave Macmillan, 2020), which was awarded Honourable Mention in the MSA First Book Award, and *Sew with Butterflies: poems* (Steel Bananas, 2014), as well as the chapbook *Spirit-clenched* (Gap Riot Press, 2020).

Maggie Wang studies at the University of Oxford. Her writing has appeared or will appear in *Poetry Wales, Borderlands: Texas Poetry Review, Bedtime Stories for the End of the World*, and elsewhere. She is a 2021 Ledbury Emerging Poetry Critic.

Susan Wardell is from Dunedin, New Zealand, where she lectures in social anthropology, while raising two small humans. Her poetry, essays, and flash fiction have been published in a variety of journals and anthologies, and she has won several international awards. She is the current poetry editor of *Anthropology and Humanism*.

Jen Webb is Distinguished Professor of Creative Practice at the University of Canberra, and co-editor of the literary journal *Meniscus*. She researches and writes about suffering and resilience. Her most recent poetry collections are *Moving Targets* (Recent Work Press, 2018), and *Flight Mode* (with Shé Hawke, Recent Work Press, 2020).

Irene Wilkie has published two books of poems, *Love and Galactic Spiders* (Ginninderra Press, 2005) and *Extravagance (*Ginninderra Press, 2013), which won a Highly Commended award in the ACT Writing and Publishing Awards 2014 for Poetry. Her work has appeared in *Divan, Going Down Swinging, Australian Poetry Journal, Australian Poetry Anthology, Award Winning Australian Writers, Flashing the Square* and *The Poetry and Place Anthology*.

Sophia Wilson's writing has appeared in various journals and anthologies. Her poetry sequence on migration was runner-up in the 2020 Kathleen Grattan Prize. She was winner of the recent Robert Burns Poetry Competition, Hippocrates Prize and Caselberg Trust International Poetry Prize. Originally from rural New South Wales, she lives in Aotearoa New Zealand with her partner and three Eurasian daughters.

Jena Woodhouse has published six poetry collections, and has been a recipient of creative residencies in Scotland, Ireland, France and Greece: a country and culture where she spent more than a decade pursuing a passion for mythology and archaeology, and a site of continuing revelation and inspiration. Distinctions include three shortlistings for the Montreal International Poetry Prize and five for the ACU Prize for Poetry.

www.ingramcontent.com/pod-product-compliance
Lightning Source LLC
Chambersburg PA
CBHW011151290426
44109CB00025B/2564